GUILT AND SIN IN TRADITIONAL CHINA

*The Second Hell.
Painting by
Hsi-chin chü-shih,
thirteenth century.
The indistinct quality
of this reproduction
is due to the condition
of the original painting.
(Metropolitan
Museum of Art,
New York)*

OF CALIFORNIA PRESS BERKELEY AND LOS ANGELES, CALIFORNIA

UNIVERSITY PRESS LONDON, ENGLAND

© 1967
NTS OF THE UNIVERSITY OF CALIFORNIA

ONGRESS CATALOG CARD NUMBER: 67–12297

IE UNITED STATES OF AMERICA

GUIL
AN
S

TRADITIO
CH

W

UNIVERSITY

CAMBRIDGE

COPYRIGHT
BY THE REG

LIBRARY OF

PRINTED IN T

UNIVERSITY OF CALIFORNIA PRE

Acknowledgments

I wish to thank most of all my wife for her critical readings and discussions of the manuscript; Mrs. Miriam Dyer-Bennet for her help in editing; Mr. Huang Yao-hsün for his assistance in reading Fukien dialect texts. Some of the research used in chapter II was done with the assistance of a Ford Foundation research grant. The typing of the manuscript was paid for by a Social Science Research grant of the University of California at Berkeley.

Contents

Introduction

Once again: Guilt or Shame?

With the growing interest in comparative sociological studies, two main lines of approach have developed. The majority of comparative sociologists, especially in the United States, assumes quietly that sociological laws or regularities found through research in the United States are of general validity and should be rediscoverable in any other society. Apparent differences should be accounted for by faulty research approaches, such as comparing data which are in themselves of different character.

A minority of sociologists, on the other hand, is of the opinion that although some of our general sociological laws may be generally valid for all human societies, some societies have specific properties that cause them to behave in specific ways and not follow the rules of behavior found in other societies. The specific character may be, for example, an economic factor, such as "irrigation economy," supposed to be typical of "Oriental societies," in contrast to "rain economy," supposed to be typical of Western societies. It is assumed that such a factor has such wide ramifications that it influences social behavior in numerous areas and produces a specific type of society for which specific laws or regularities have to be found.

In the 1920's, psychological theories were developed which attempted to explain the supposedly basic differences between different groups of societies. Societies have been divided into categories, such as cultures characterized by logic and thinking versus others based on "pre-logic" (Levy-Bruhl and others), or those ruled by "homo faber" against those ruled by "homo magicus" (Theodor W. Danzel). While the early psychological theories tried to differentiate between "primitive" and "civilized" societies, later psychological theories have repeatedly attempted to

1

explain the cultural differences between the great civilizations of the East—usually China and/or India, more rarely Japan—and the civilizations of the West.

One of these theories goes back to a statement by Sigmund Freud concerning the importance of the "sense of guilt" for the evolution of culture.[1] It was pointed out that the concept of guilt has been very important in Western civilization, and that the socialization of children was achieved mainly by sensitizing them to the feeling of guilt. On the other hand, it has been stated by various authors that socialization in the Far East, especially in China, Japan, and Burma, was performed mainly by instilling a feeling for shame (according to Francis L. K. Hsu, Erik Erikson, Hazel Hitson). Thus "guilt societies" were contrasted with "shame societies."

The agency which produces either feelings of shame or feelings of guilt is, according to these scholars, the family. In a society in which the child is trained either by a number of socializing agents (as may be the case in an extended family) or in which the trainers discipline the child by saying that he will be punished by other social agents, "shame-oriented" personality types are produced. The individual is afraid of a withdrawal of the love of others,[2] of being suddenly out of key with his environment,[3] of not meeting the trust that he has in himself.[4] As most nonindustrial societies are strongly hierarchically structured, the child in such a society feels himself the recipient of action by someone in authority, with no initial responsibility toward others and no influence upon the way others act toward him.[5] The most important thing is to avoid shame and anger from others. There is anxiety about punishment that might come if one has unwittingly offended others,[6] a punishment which carries with it implications of social ostracism and possible destruction.[7] The individual has internalized the norms of the socializing agents, but what seems to be internalized are "ought-nots": [8] one ought not let oneself be shamed by others, one ought not make authority figures angry.

On the other hand, in societies in which the child is trained by only a few agents of socialization (as is the case in a nuclear family) which

---

[1] Sigmund Freud, *Civilization and Its Discontents* (New York, 1930), p. 123.

[2] Melford E. Spiro, "Social Systems, Personality, and Functional Analysis," in Bert Kaplan, ed., *Studying Personality Cross-culturally* (Evanston, 1961).

[3] Helen M. Lynd, *On Shame and the Search for Identity* (New York, 1961), p. 35.

[4] *Ibid.*, p. 209.

[5] Hazel Hitson, "Family Patterns and Paranoidal Personality Structure in Boston and Burma" (unpublished Ph.D dissertation, Radcliffe College, 1959), p. 192.

[6] *Ibid.*, p. 183.

[7] *Ibid.*, p. 154.

[8] *Ibid.*, p. 180.

themselves administer punishments, the children internalize the social norms as well as introject the socializing agent.[9] In this situation, punishment for transgressions is experienced as guilt. Guilt is wrongdoing, an actual and tangible violation of sanctions,[10] often coupled with a feeling of remorse or regret. In such societies, the child is expected to assume responsibility for his own actions, and when there is failure in any way, self-blame follows.[11] The child is responsible for the way others behave and feel toward him.[12] A guilt-oriented person feels guilt when he transgresses, even if no one around him notices his transgression, because the agent of punishment is always in him.[13]

If the concepts of guilt and shame are defined in this way, it is tempting to correlate them with specific types of cultures. "Primitive" cultures, it is said, achieve socialization with more emphasis upon shame and develop a morality which is dominantly centered in the family and in the face-to-face group,[14] while literate and urban cultures give increased importance to internalized self-responsibility. In urban cultures, the moral order is derived more or less exclusively from the parents, whereas in nonliterate societies with extended families, a great number of family members and even outsiders may be crucial in the "incorporation of the superego." [15] This dichotomy can easily be correlated with David Riesman's "tradition-directed" and "inner-directed" societies.[16]

It is admitted by the proponents of this theory that there are hardly any pure "shame" or pure "guilt" cultures, that shame and guilt both are utilized to ensure socialization of the individual,[17] and if a culture is called a "shame" culture this should only indicate that shame is a more prominent agent than guilt, not an absence of guilt. Japanese culture, for instance, has often been regarded as a shame culture on the basis of early studies.[18] George DeVos, however, came to the conclusion that the strong achievement drive, found in Japanese TAT (Thematic Apperception Test) responses, not only is a shame-oriented concern with community standards, but is linked with an undercurrent of guilt. He believes that guilt in Japan is not linked with supernatural sanctions (sin), but is

[9] Spiro, *op. cit.* (see n. 2 above), p. 120.
[10] Carrington M. Lowe, "The Study of the Nature of Guilt in Psychopathology," *Dissertation Abstracts*, Vol. 22 (1961), pp. 909–910.
[11] Hitson, *op. cit.,* p. 179
[12] *Ibid.,* p. 192.
[13] Spiro, *op. cit.* (see n. 2 above), p. 120.
[14] Clyde Kluckhohn, "The Moral Order in the Expanding Society," in C. H. Kraeling and R. M. Adams, *City Invincible* (Chicago, 1960), p. 397.
[15] *Ibid.*
[16] Margaret L. Cormack, *She Who Rides a Peacock* (New York, 1961), pp. 232–233.
[17] Kluckhohn, *op. cit.,* p. 397.
[18] Ruth Benedict, *The Chrysanthemum and the Sword* (London, 1947).

derived from a system of loyalties in the traditional Japanese society [19] and is linked to the nature of interpersonal relationships within the family, especially the mother-child relationship.

As Chinese society certainly falls into the "tradition-directed" type, and as its ideal is the extended family, it can easily be seen that social psychologists have regarded Chinese society as a "shame society." Attention was called to such expressions as "to lose face" (*shih-lien*) where face (*lien*) refers to personal integrity, good character, and the confidence of society and of oneself in one's ability to play one's social role.[20] A person "loses face" if he does not live up to the expectations set for his role, if he breaks rules of conduct. He is, then, punished with ridicule, contempt, or social ostracism. The reaction of society is not only directed against the culprit but may reflect back upon his family, sometimes even upon his ancestry. This concept of shame implies, as stated by Helen M. Lynd,[21] the acceptance of the validity of the basic values of the society and is a "conservative" agent. Conservatism has often been regarded as a typical trait of traditional Chinese society.

National Character

Any statement concerning characteristics of a total society, or the "national character," has to be specified. Geoffrey Gorer has shown that the concept of national character has several meanings.[22] According to him, it may refer to the principal motives or predispositions which can be deduced from the behavior of the members of a society. Studies of this aspect will often be statistical in character and will make use of tests; the study on Japan mentioned above is of this kind.

"National character" can also mean the ideal image which a society has of itself, according to Gorer. It is possible to conduct studies along these lines in part by means of questionnaires. In addition, various literary sources could be used, including legal, moralistic, nationalistic, and often also religious literature, which directly or indirectly depict the "ideal person" as it should be but as it rarely is.

Thirdly, one could study the means which a society uses to instill and

[19] E. Norbeck and G. DeVos, "Japan," in Francis L. K. Hsu, ed., *Psychological Anthropology* (Homewood, 1961), pp. 19–47.

[20] Hu Hsien-chin, "The Chinese Concept of Face," in *American Anthropologist,* Vol. 46 (1944), pp. 45–66.

[21] Lynd, *loc. cit.* (see n. 3 above).

[22] Margaret Mead and R. Métraux, *Study of Culture at a Distance* (New York, 1953), p. 57.

to maintain certain motives and predispositions. This would largely be a study of the social institutions of the society. Institutions and their mechanisms of enforcement are ways of channeling social needs in specific ways. They aim at creating predispositions for certain ways of behavior, but it is understood that not all individuals, perhaps not even always the majority, will really act according to these predispositions. A statistical study in this field is hardly possible.[23] The main sources would be the legal codes of the society and the books on etiquette and behavior.

The first approach would establish the actual value-system of the members of a society; the last approach, the ideal value-system of the individual members of the society. The second approach, however, would bring forth the picture which the members of a society have of themselves as a collectivity, as a nation.

All studies of national character, in whatever way it is defined, are quite difficult in stratified traditional societies. We must take into consideration the fact that different social classes or social layers have different value-systems. In the case of China, it has been clearly expressed that the value-system set up by the Confucian classics is the ideal image of and for the upper class, the elite. This elite hoped that the lower classes could be educated gradually toward the ideal, but did not expect full compliance. If, therefore, we were to make a statistical study of the "predispositions" of *the* Chinese on the basis of actual behavior, we would get the predispositions of the majority of the Chinese, that is, the lower classes, and such a study would exhibit little of "Confucian ideals," [24] as they may not be fully aware of the value-system of the elite. Such studies in themselves are highly interesting; obviously they cannot be done today in mainland China. It is also impossible to do a historical study of this topic on the basis of textual material because texts, usually written by members of the elite, report overwhelmingly the actual behavior of the upper, and not of the lower, classes.

Studies attempting to find the ideal image that Chinese have of themselves are fairly numerous; many of the studies on "the Chinese family" are of this type. As the ideals of a society are normally formulated by the elite, the picture emerging from these studies is that of the Confucianist Chinese. These studies often start with an analysis of books of ceremonies (such as the *Li-chi, I-li,* etc.), or their analysis of customs is

---

[23] One could ask questions like "How should one act in this situation?" of a sample of the upper class and educators. The lower classes may not be conscious of the institutions. Attitude questions like "How would you act in this situation?" would not give the same result.

[24] I mean here surveys in which people were asked: "How did you act in this situation?"

consciously or unconsciously influenced by these books. But are these books really the means by which "predispositions and motives" of the lower classes are instilled or maintained? A Chinese scholar, writing around 1700,[25] has clearly indicated that this was not necessarily so. He compares the six classics, the compendium of the ideal values of the elite, with folk literature, the means of instilling values in the lower classes:

When I look at the common man, I find nobody who does not love to sing songs and to see plays. These are "The Book of Songs" and "The Book of Music" of natural man. There is none who does not read novels or listen to story-tellers. These are the "Book of History" and the "Spring and Autumn Annals" of the natural man. There is none who does not believe in oracles and who does not sacrifice to spirits and gods. These are the "Book of Changes" and the "Book of Rites" of the natural man. Once, I discussed with Han T'u-lin the dramas and novels of our time. Mr. Han believed that they spoiled man's heart more than anything else. One should strictly prohibit them. I said: "Sir, do not say so. Dramas and novels are the great pivot by which the wise king turns and changes the world. If the saints would rise again, they would not reign without them."

Here, Mr. Han represents the orthodox Confucianist, while our author believes that the folk literature, through songs, plays, novels, stories, and superstitions, expresses values in the form in which the common man can understand them and that folk literature acts among the masses as the means to create and to maintain "predispositions" which, though not as lofty as those of the elite, are still valuable. Moreover, folk literature, he believes, can be used as a vehicle for slowly transforming the values of the masses. A systematic and comprehensive study of the values implicit in the folk literature has not yet been undertaken.

Aims and Limits of the Investigation

This book on guilt and sin belongs in the third group of studies mentioned above. It is based on Chinese literary documents; it is not a psychological study and does not include a general analysis. I have refrained from using a psychoanalytical or any other Western psychological frame of reference for the concepts of guilt and shame.

Several studies—which I do not want to criticize here—have postulated that Chinese society is a shame society, in contrast to Western guilt society. I believe that not enough attention has been devoted to the

[25] *Kuang-yang tsa-chi* 2, 31a.

occurrence and the meaning of "guilt" in China, and therefore—more specifically—I wanted to find out the role of the concepts of guilt and sin in the different strata of Chinese premodern society. I do not assume a priori that Chinese society is characterized by a more or less distinctive basic or modal personality type.[26] I also do not assume that cultural integration in China has brought about consistency in the folk material, although I think that there is very little reliable material which really represents the "folk," such as folktales, folk songs, perhaps legends and myths. Most of the "folk" material is not written *by*, but is written *for*, the masses, such as novels, plays, educational or moralistic pamphlets.

I was interested in the ways by which the concepts of guilt and sin have been implanted in the minds of the Chinese masses, though it was not possible to establish to what degree the masses at any period of history had internalized these values. I was also interested to see how educated Chinese evaluated and judged behavior. Did they judge it in terms of guilt and sin or in terms of shame? Did they judge it equally for the elite and for the masses, or did they make a difference? In short, I wanted to study, in the main, what the Chinese have said or thought about sin and guilt.

Two problems came up in working with these literary documents. It has been asserted that literature serves needs for which society has not provided public outlets.[27] Specifically, myths presumably project needs which are overtly denied and repressed and for whose handling the society has few or no institutions. From our knowledge of Chinese literature, this does not apply to the literature used in this study, namely short stories and moralistic treatises. It may to some degree be true for certain popular novels and folktales, and especially for jokes.

The other problem is whether the stories and treatises conceal latent meanings which differ from the manifest meaning and whether they can be analyzed within the frame of psychoanalytical symbolism. The short stories, for instance, are not fantasies of their authors. They are descriptions of happenings or supposed events which took place or were believed to have actually taken place, although they do not necessarily describe typical or normal events. As many an author has emphasized, the author wrote a story because he considered an event interesting or significant—we might add, within the framework of his and his reader's social values—and he expected the same reaction from his readers. Of course, the short stories are colored by the writer's aesthetic or literary preferences and by his personal psychological situation. If one knows the

[26] Cf. Victor Barnouw, *Culture and Personality* (Homewood, 1963), p. 306.
[27] Melville Jacobs, *The Content and Style of an Oral Literature* (New York, 1959), p. 130.

life history of an author and analyzes the hundreds of short stories which
he has written, one may gain some insight into his personal psychology,
but still one will have no means to establish the degree to which his
personal psychology may have influenced an individual story. However,
whatever the authors describe, their stories contain, besides individual
values, internalized values which are shared by the authors and their
readers. An important means of communicating these values is the
symbolism provided by the culture. Without any doubt, as long as we do
not understand the meaning of all symbols used by the writer and
commonly known in his time, we cannot even attempt to establish the
latent meaning of a story in psychoanalytical terms.

Let me illustrate this problem, in order to clarify my position. There is
a widely known southern Chinese folktale with the following main
motifs: Virgins carry a certain disease (usually leprosy) which they
transfer to the first man with whom they have intercourse. If they do not
transfer the disease, they must die of it. The first man also must die; the
girl then marries a second man. In the tale the girl explains the situation
to the unsuspecting first man and only pretends intercourse with him,
because they fell in love with one another and she did not want him to
die. The man returns home and marries a wife, while the girl becomes ill,
confesses, and is driven out of her home. She finally finds the man, who
takes her into his home, houses her in a special, separate room, where
she expects to die from the disease. In her desperation and pain she
drinks a pot of wine into which a snake had fallen, hoping to be killed by
the poison. However, the poison of the snake heals her, so that she can
finally marry the man as his second wife.[28]

This story was taken as a typical example of the fear of sexual
intercourse which was said to be characteristic of Chinese men.[29] However, this story is known only in a small part of China, mainly Kuangtung province. It is connected with customs of premarital freedom and
high status of women occurring in these non-Chinese tribal societies,
which existed and in part still exist in the area.[30] The story may be
characteristic for these non-Chinese tribes; certainly it is not characteristic for all Chinese; and even though some Chinese tell this story, we can
by no means be sure that retelling this unusual tale expresses their own
sexual attitudes. Moreover, it is quite possible that the motif of the

[28] Discussion of this type of folktale in Wolfram Eberhard, *Typen chinesischer
Volksmärchen* (Helsinki, 1937), Type No. 197, and *Volksmärchen aus Südost-
China* (Helsinki, 1941), pp. 215–216.

[29] V. Heyer, "Relations Between Men and Women in China," in Margaret Mead
and R. Métraux, *Study of Culture at a Distance*, p. 225.

[30] These customs are analyzed in Wolfram Eberhard, *Die Lokalkulturen im
alten China* (Peking, 1943), Vol. 2.

"poison-damsel" reached South China by diffusion [31] and expressed sexual attitudes of another, quite distant society. The healing of the dying by poisonous wine, too, is an international motif. In Chinese folk literature it is unique, not typical. Therefore, this motif can hardly be used to draw conclusions on the Chinese national character. Wine in China is normally not red and, therefore, for the Chinese, not reminiscent of blood. Nor is any fluid in a bowl necessarily a sexual symbol for the Chinese,[32] because the typical Chinese way to treat a sick person is to give him medicine to drink from a bowl, whatever the disease might be. And in most versions of the tale, the girl does not drink from the bowl but directly from the jug.

In another story, the monk Mu-lien had just retrieved his mother from the hells into which she had fallen because of her numerous sins.[33] When he was walking with her, she pulled a turnip out of a field and ate it, whereupon Mu-lien cut off his finger and planted it in place of the turnip. The story concludes that since then turnips are red. Eating a carrot or turnip is not forbidden by religion,[34] but pulling the turnip in this story was a simple act of theft, a new sin. The story does not mean to show the monk's devotion to his mother; it is a typical Buddhist moralistic tale, whose origin is India, praising the virtues of a good monk. Self-mutilation is utterly abhorrent to the Chinese, and classical texts (*Hsiao-ching*) condemned it as a violation of filial piety. The story propagandizes non-Chinese virtues and values of a foreign religion and does not reflect Chinese feeling. Besides, the turnip should not, because of its form, be taken as symbolizing a phallus, unless there are further indications. Typically Chinese (non-Buddhist) stories dwell on the smell of some turnips and connect them with feces, not with phalli.[35] There are, indeed, stories in which a sixth finger is cut off,[36] but it is utterly doubtful whether for a Chinese this symbolizes castration. The stress, for

[31] See Norman M. Penzer, *Poison-damsels and other Essays* (London, 1952), pp. 36–71. Penzer shows the possible relation to the *vagina dentata* motif which is known from India (see also Verrier Elwin, *Myths of Middle India* [Oxford, 1949], pp. 354ff.), Taiwan (Wang Sung-hsing in *Bulletin of the Institute of Ethnology*, No. 14 [1962], pp. 112–113, and Ho Ting-jui, "East Asian Themes in Folktales of the Formosan Aborigines," in *Asian Folklore Studies*, Vol. 23 [1964], No. 2, pp. 43–45), North America, and other places.

[32] V. Heyer, *loc. cit.*

[33] This story will be mentioned later. The tale is W. Eberhard, *Typen*, No. 89. It is not a very common tale.

[34] V. Heyer thinks so. *Op. cit.*, p. 226.

[35] W. Eberhard, *Typen*, No. 89b.

[36] V. Heyer, *loc. cit.* The story is in *Liao-chai chih-i* 2. I do not know any further stories of a sixth finger. This story is also analyzed by W. Muensterberger in "Orality and Dependence: Characteristics of Southern Chinese," in *Psychoanalysis and the Social Sciences*, Vol. 3, pp. 37–69. Muensterberger is more cautious than Heyer in his general conclusions.

the Chinese, is on the sixth, supernumerary, finger, not on the self-mutilation: it exists against the laws of nature, which are based on the number five, and cutting it off reestablishes the balance of nature.

These two examples show another problem, which is typical for folktales and legends but not for the short stories. Folktales and legends often have centuries of literary history behind them. Even if we assume that at the time of their origin they expressed a certain latent attitude or value of the society, can we assume that, centuries later, the society still has the same attitudes and values and still continues to express them through the same symbols or through the same tale? Before a psychoanalytical analysis of material from China can become fruitful, we have to know the literary clichés which writers in each century used; the common symbols (often puns) which the language used in each century [37] and by which a meaning—but not a latent one—is expressed; the personality of the writer; the region from which the information comes, because different parts of China had and often still have different languages (and therefore different symbols), culture, and social structure. It is for these reasons that I have refrained from psychoanalytical interpretations which often seem so "obvious" to some of us. One could certainly be more courageous if there were enough empirical studies of Chinese social psychology which were also scientifically satisfactory. For our purposes, studies of the family and of the socialization of children would probably be most important. However, thus far, almost all existing studies of such topics take their information from traditional Chinese literature or from statements by Chinese made on the basis of ideals taken from the same books [38] and not from systematic observation or from tests applied to Chinese from all walks of life in all areas of China.

Plan of Study

In the following chapters we shall examine the concepts of "sin" and "guilt," first by showing the connection between transgression and punishment, or, in other words, which acts were believed to be punishable

[37] Take for instance the bat: the Chinese does not connect it with the night or with vampires, but for him a pun is involved. The bat (*fu*) means luck (*fu*). Any interpretation of the occurrence of a bat in a dream or in a story has to start from this pun.

[38] This is also true for the generalizations in Francis L. K. Hsu, *Clan, Caste, and Club* (New York, 1963), although Hsu, one of the first to set up the shame/guilt dichotomy, also has done fieldwork (as in "Some Aspects of Personality of Chinese as Revealed by the Rorschach Test," in *Rorschach Research Exchange* and *Journal of Projective Techniques,* Vol. 13 [1949], No. 3, pp. 285–301).

by supernatural powers and what were the punishments. Secondly, we will see whether such ideas have changed in China over the centuries.

Our main sources are some of the so-called *shan-shu,* books for moral improvement, which are printed and distributed by persons who, by the act of propagating the books, acquire religious "merit" which, after death, will delete wrong acts and add to the sum of good acts. Such books are extremely common, even in today's Taiwan. Parts of such books are found also in popular almanacs in pre-Communist China; they were found in almost every house. It is true that educated Chinese looked down upon this type of literature (and therefore our libraries do not like to collect them). The producers of *shan-shu* are very conscious and scornful of this attitude and try to show, by giving numerous examples, that even scholars would do well to believe in the precepts given in the *shan-shu.* They usually add a number of stories in which scholars were "converted." But even if the majority of scholars may have had the same attitude toward these books as educated Westerners may show toward simple religious tracts, their mothers—we can be sure—knew these texts and were influenced by them.

CHAPTER ONE

The Concept of Sin in Chinese Folk Religion

The Chinese Terms

Before we begin the main discussion, a word should be said about the Chinese terms for guilt and shame. As we will later show in more detail, the problem is easy for "guilt": the term is the same as the word for "crime" and also for "sin." Guilt–crime–sin are one chain. The problem is more difficult for the concept "shame," which already in English contains two different meanings (expressed clearly in German: *Scham/Schande*). The most common Chinese term *ch'ih* is written with the determinant "ear" and the word for "heart" and is explained by lexicographers as a feeling which causes one's ears to become red. In this connection it may be interesting to note that psychologists tend to see a correlation of shame with visual exposure and of guilt with auditory admonition.[1] There is no Chinese word denoting shame which refers to visual exposure.[2] *Ju* with the meaning "disgrace," seems to have had the original meaning of "to dirty," while *hsiu*, with the meaning "shame," seems to stem from the same root as *ju*, with an additional connotation of "ugly." The word which is most commonly used in colloquial Chinese, *ts'an-k'ui*, meaning "ashamed," has most clearly the basic meaning of "ugly." It is now highly interesting that the first word for "ugly" seems to

[1] Helen Lynd, *On Shame and the Search for Identity* (New York, 1961), p. 207.

[2] It is interesting, however, that the word *yen*, which in classical Chinese is the word often used to express "loss of face," has in addition to the main meaning of "face" also the connotation of "color" and, derived from this connotation, the second connotation, "sex." The second word for sex, *sê*, also has the basic meaning of "color." Both words clearly refer to impressions of the eye. The sexual act, however, has the connotation of flowing water (*yin*).

have had the connotation of "bad smell," while the second word has the connotation of "smelling, dirty" (*wei*). This same word "dirty" was used in the fifth century A.D. by Buddhists to denote "sin." Correspondingly, the term *lien-hsin*, "bashful," has the basic meaning of "clean heart." The Buddhist "paradise," the place in which there is no sin, is called *ching-t'u*, "clean land."

This brief philological excursion indicates then two important traits: (1) the concept of shame has the connotation of "dirty," "smelly." From other studies, it became clear that "dirt" has the connotation of "blood," "pus." Shame in Chinese has no connotation related to visual exposure, nor to a loss of acceptance by society. (2) The connotations of words for shame are the same as the connotations of "sin." We will later see how close the connotations of "sin" are to "unclean," especially to blood and pus.

In our Western thinking, we can define "sin" as a violation of rules belonging to a moral code set up and guarded by the supernatural, that is, by personal deities or by supernatural but unpersonal powers. We differentiate clearly between sin and crime: generally speaking, all crimes are sin, but not all sins are crime. Sin is more inclusive than crime. The Chinese do not use different terms. The same words that are used in social contexts are used in religious contexts. *Tsui* has three basic meanings: crime, punishment of a crime, and sin. The other key term, *kuo,* means a criminal act which has been unintentionally committed, as well as a sin which has been committed without any intention. All crimes (*tsui* and *kuo*) are sins, but not all violations of the moral code set up by the deities are crimes and punished by the laws of the realm.

Shame, Sin, and Guilt

In my attempts to find documentary material in Chinese sources for a study of shame, I was astonished to find few texts which undoubtedly referred to shame. Even a body of over fifteen hundred short stories which I studied yielded but few data. Yet we know very well that the concept of shame always existed and still exists. From the many references to shame in discussions of modern Chinese society, we even got the impression that shame today, or in the nineteenth century, played an even stronger role than in earlier times. In a number of cases in which we would expect an evaluation in terms of shame, we find an evaluation in terms of sin or guilt, and shame occurs only if the action is made publicly known. Therefore, the main topic of this study is a study

of sin. Sin was defined as actions, behavior, and thoughts that violated
rules set up by supernatural powers. Sin is the equivalent of legal guilt,
which is a violation of rules set up by earthly powers and the emotion
which results from such a violation of legal rules. We might say that
persons who have such a concept of "sin," and the emotions accompanying a sinful act or thought, seem to have internalized social norms to a
perhaps even higher degree than persons who have only a feeling for
legal guilt, because Chinese supernatural rules are based upon social
norms. They are not in contradiction to these social norms and laws but
strengthen and tighten them.

In contrast to the meager information on shame, there is in China an
extremely extensive literature which deals with sin. We can be fairly sure
that while not everybody believed in what the books say about sin and
the punishment of sins, many, and even many well-educated persons, at
least in certain stages of their life, believed in it. In this literature about
sin, we find clear statements which stress the responsibility of the individual for his actions:

> Whoever does good deeds without expecting rewards, belongs to the
> highest class of people. Whoever does a good deed because he expects a
> reward, belongs to the medium class of people. But whoever knows about
> rewards and yet cannot do good, or even turns to bad actions, belongs to the
> lowest type of people.[3]
> Misfortune or good luck have no need for doors—man himself calls them
> in. The rewards for good and bad are like the shadow which follows the
> object. Therefore, heaven and earth have spirits who control violations.
> According to the importance of a violation, they take away from the account
> of a person: if the account is decreased, he will be poor; he will meet with
> much grief and suffering; other people will despise him. Punishment and
> misfortune will always be after him, and good luck will stay away from him.
> Bad stars will ruin him. And when his account is exhausted, he will die. Then
> there are also the spirits of the Three Terraces [4] and the Northern Bushel,
> who record above the head of a person his sins and take days away from his
> life-span. In addition, there are the three personal spirits, inside the human
> body, who on every fifty-seventh day (of a sixty-day cycle) go up to see the
> heavenly offices and report on the sins of the person. And on every last day
> of the month, the god of the hearth does the same. . . .[5]

This text, as well as many others, makes it clear that the Chinese did
not believe in a blind fate, that the individual was responsible for his
fate, and that his actions, even though they may remain unknown to

---

[3] *T'ai-shang pao-fa t'u-shuo.* Preface of 1735 by Ho Yü-lin, p. 4b.

[4] The Three Terraces (*san-t'ai*) and the Northern Bushel (*pei-tou*) are constel-
lations.

[5] *T'ai-shang pao-fa t'u-shuo.* Introduction, p. 22a (a quotation from *T'ai shang
kan-ying p'ien*).

society, are known to the deities and receive punishment (or reward?).[6] We will later see that the Chinese did not always have such a concept of sin, and that it developed fairly late in Chinese history.

In addition to such feelings of sin, feelings of guilt must have been associated also with the violations or transgressions in the field of social relations—that is, social role behavior—most of which were punishable by human law and all of which, according to popular religion, led to punishment in the hereafter. The Burmese, who have been described as having a shame-culture,[7] also know "guilt": they believe in spirits, the *nat,* which are simply an extension of the human social hierarchy to a higher level and are continuous with it.[8] In order to get a concession from them, one has to make them a gift, that is, a sacrifice. But just as persons of high social status in Burma can easily be offended, there is a persistent anxiety in Burma that one might have made the *nat* angry and that they might react even more violently than human superiors.[9] Similar beliefs can be found in popular Chinese attitudes toward religion: the deities are only an extension of human society into the supernatural realm. They have to be pacified, just as a high official has to be "softened" by a gift. They may become angry and cause terrible harm to the person who made them angry. But—and this is different from Burma—Chinese deities may also "sin" and be punished by still higher deities for such sins, deities as well as human beings are subject to the same moral laws.

A drama of the Ming period [10] gives a very good illustration for this point. A family because of poverty handed their daughter over to a god by putting her into his temple. The god wanted to retain the girl and to rape her. A scholar who had heard of this case, denied the god the right to do this and, as the god did not react, fought with the god and wounded him. He saved the girl and later had the god degraded in rank

---

[6] Guilt is internalized and works in a person whether or not others know about his actions (John J. Honigman, *Understanding Culture* [New York, 1963], p. 245). Correspondingly, Chinese believed that deities punish sinful intentions even if the act has not been committed: "Although the action did not take place, he had in fact the intention to commit it" and therefore received punishment (*T'ai-shang pao-fa t'u-shuo,* 5, 45b).

[7] Hazel Hitson, "Family Patterns and Paranoidal Personality Structure in Boston and Burma" (unpublished Ph.D. dissertation, Radcliffe College, 1959), *passim.*

[8] Edmund R. Leach, *Political Systems of Highland Burma* (Cambridge, England, 1954), p. 173. I do not define this as guilt.

[9] Hitson, *op. cit.,* p. 184.

[10] *Wan shih tsu* (*Ch'ü-hai,* I, 422–425). I want to remark here that such references to single "stories" are included in this study only as illustrations and not as "proofs."

by an imperial order of the Chinese emperor. To violate a girl that has been given in trust is a sin, even for a god.

Sin in Chinese Folk Religion

If we apply our definition of "sin"—a violation of a divine code— Chinese folk religion before the Han period (206 B.C.) seems not to have had the concept of sin, although it recognized a great number of supernatural beings. People who offended the deities, spirits, or other supernatural beings by not honoring them or by failing to sacrifice in the right way or at the right time might make them angry. The deities then could or would punish such people. An event of this kind was more or less like any offense against a human superior, with the only difference that deities were believed to be superior to humans; they formed, if this expression be permitted, a social class above the upper class in human society. This class of supernatural beings was structured: some deities had more, others less, power, but the structure was more like a class structure than like a bureaucratic one although one god was vaguely recognized as the highest of all.

Law codes governing the humans were created several centuries before Christ, but whether these codes were applied in court, and if so, whether they applied to all men or only to some groups is doubtful. Similarly, each deity personally punished the humans who had made him angry, according to the god's own judgment and character and in an arbitrary way, without reference to a code. The wrath of a deity could be assuaged by appropriate ceremonies; still better, man could avoid the divine wrath by giving the deity what it expected and wanted. These beliefs express what might be called an oligarchic absolutism; deities were numerous, they acted as they pleased and were not even always of good character.

Philosophers as well as the general population believed that man has two souls. One was an impersonal, life-sustaining "body soul," while the other was a personal soul which made an individual out of a human being. The general belief was that at the time of death both souls continued to live in some way. The body soul remained close to the body and—if the body was treated correctly—slowly decayed. The personal soul continued to live. Many people seem to have thought that this soul would live approximately as long as any living person still remembered the departed one. And many seem to have believed that the personal soul continued to live near the home, perhaps even in the ancestral figure or (later) ancestral tablet which was kept in the ancestral temple or in the home. But others clearly believed that the personal souls would go to a high mountain and live there.[11] Still others must have believed that the souls would live in another world below our own world, a world of shadow, a world in which everything is opposite to what it is in our world.[12] There were no ideas of judgment and punishment after death.[13]

Philosophers of the time avoided the discussion of the supernatural. They set up an ethical system based not upon relations to the supernatural but on something that today we might call "human nature." In modern terms, we would call their system a system of social ethics aiming to achieve a peaceful coexistence of many individuals in a narrow space. Many actions which they condemned as unethical were still quite common but not yet regarded as crimes and not yet punished by law.

Buddhism spread in China at the latest from the first century A.D. on. It brought a whole set of new concepts. We are interested here, not in philosophical Buddhism, but rather in folk Buddhism, a simplified form which even the uneducated could understand. It seems that folk Buddhism almost immediately brought to China the concept of sin and of punishment of sin. Texts, which are attributed to the late second century A.D., already enumerated the punishments meted out to the souls of sinners in different "hells." [14] A sin committed during a lifetime was not immediately punished, but the sinner received punishment after death. This was an attempt to answer the eternal question why some people who had committed many crimes or immoral acts had a good life until

[11] Wolfram Eberhard, *Die Lokalkulturen im alten China,* Vol. 1, pp. 260–261.

[12] See texts such as *Yo-ming-lu,* quoted in *T'ai-p'ing kuang-chi,* 379, Vol. 30, 44b; *Min-pao-chi,* quoted in *ibid.,* 42b; *Ho-tung-chi,* quoted in *ibid.,* 384, Vol. 31, 20b; et cetera. For a general discussion see W. Mühlmann in *Kölner Zeitschr. für Soziologie,* Vol. 13 (1961), No. 4, pp. 614–624.

[13] The Sih-ming (Controller of Fate) is known as an official of the other world who keeps the lists and controls men and spirits. He can call people to his place and act as a judge; he can end a man's life or even bring a person back to life. Later texts identify him either with the god of the hearth (see Wilhelm Grube, *Pekinger Volkskunde,* p. 61) or with a judge of hell. What exactly his function and character were before Buddhism came to China is not clear. He is mentioned in pre-Han texts, which give the impression that he is an official who deals out punishments and rewards as officials on earth do. Holmes Welch, in *Taoism: The Parting of the Way* (Boston, 1966), p. 100, refers to a line in the *Shu-ching* which seems to indicate that this deity kept records of righteousness. It is possible that here we have a belief which comes close to a belief in sin.

[14] *Fo-shuo shih-pa ni-li ching,* Text No. 731. *Taishô Tripitaka,* Vol. 17, p. 528b; and *Fo-shuo tsui-yeh ying-pao chiao-hua ti-yü ching,* Text No. 724, *Taishô Tripitaka,* Vol. 17, p. 450c. Although the Chinese term for "hell" is *ti-yü*—earth prison or "prison below the earth"—the translation as "purgatory" might be more correct, as the *ti-yü* is a place where most sinners stay only temporarily. But as they are not completely "purged" in the *ti-yü,* and as some sinners remain eternally in it, we continue to use the traditional translation as "hell."

their death, escaping punishment by human justice. Pre-Buddhist ethics had no answer to this problem other than to refer to fate (*ming*) as an unclear, inscrutable power. The other eternal question, why persons who always behaved well sometimes met with a terrible or early death, seems to have been of less interest. Firstly, there was always the possibility that such persons had committed bad sins that had remained unknown to others. Secondly, the Buddhist doctrine of reincarnation offered an explanation: such persons are receiving punishment for acts committed in an earlier incarnation, acts of such severity that even the punishment in hell, which they already had endured, had not been sufficient. Actually, this explanation seems not to have been overly stressed in popular Buddhism, probably because its strict application would have led to full determinism, thus wiping out the responsibility of the individual for his actions. Nevertheless, the doctrine of reincarnation was used in folk Buddhism to explain why people are born into miserable social conditions in which they have to remain for their whole life, or why some people are born with congenital diseases or disabilities, without even having had a chance to commit a sin which could explain the condition.

The folk-Buddhistic concept of sin did not refer to an action against a single deity or to the provocation of divine anger, but it meant a violation of a moral code which was somehow set, and was applicable to and valid for the world of the gods as well as the world of man. Even if human justice had dealt with the criminal according to the law of the society, his offense still remained to be punished. Folk Buddhism eliminated the caprices or arbitrary reactions of deities, and instituted a religious system that we might call *constitutional monarchism,* that is, the belief in a law that is absolutely binding even for the judge and is administered in an impersonal manner by an appointed heavenly judge. In contrast to conditions in this world, in the other-world's hall of judgment there is no consideration of social class, status, sex, or age. Every person is treated mechanically according to the law. Typically, the "hall of judgment" is one of the establishments which we called "hell" above. The Chinese term *yü* means (1) a lawsuit about a criminal matter, not a financial matter, (2) a prison, (3) a hall of judgment and of punishment in a world under our world. In this meaning, the term can be clarified by adding *ti,* "earth" (*ti-yü*). A Chinese prison is not only a place in which suspects are kept before their trial or in which the convicted criminals are kept; it is a place of torture and misery as well. Few people remained alive if they had to stay long in a prison. Thus, the use of the same term for "prison" and for "hell" is logical.

The Buddhist concept of sin and judgment involves, logically, a feeling of guilt. Typically again, the term for this feeling is *tsui,* the same word as for crime. The sinner knows that his actions may remain unknown to others, but they are known to the supernatural powers and will receive punishment. No bribery, no attempt to cheat, no attempt to use social status and influence will help. Punishment will come after death, and it will be horrible. There is no way to make a sin undone. The only hope is that by doing good works a certain balance between sins and meritorious acts may be established, so that sins are outweighed by merits. In later popular belief, the procedure is similar to bookkeeping in business, where expenditures and receipts are written in different columns. Correspondingly, there is a heavenly account book in which the sins are the expenditures and the good deeds the receipts. The sinner with a negative balance sheet is punished—he is like a bankrupt merchant. Other popular concepts use the symbol of the scales on which good and bad deeds are weighed and balanced. We know of many faithful persons who did thousands of acts of merit. It may be assumed that it was not only fear of a negative balance but also guilt feelings that drove them to build pagodas, to feed monks, to give alms, to make pilgrimages.

Alongside these exacting supernatural laws leading to individual guilt, Buddhism in China had a concept of grace that had little or nothing to do with guilt. This combination occurred only within certain movements during certain periods of Chinese history. We might say that folk Buddhism during the fifth and sixth centuries, with its belief that the Savior, Maitreya (Mi-lo), would come or was already coming to save the few selected who believed in him and to destroy all others, contained this element of belief in grace. Similarly, from Mongol times on, and especially during the Ming dynasty (thirteenth to sixteenth centuries), a number of different "secret religions" had this "messianic" character and believed that mere belief in the deity and observance of a few specific divine orders was sufficient to bring about salvation, in spite of sins one might have committed. The rise of the *Ch'ing-t'u* (Pure Land) sect and similar sects in Buddhism proper during the T'ang time (seventh to tenth centuries) is another example of belief in divine grace. A follower, whether or not he had committed sins, was believed to be saved by the deity and to be brought into the "Western Paradise" without judgment of his deeds. These messianic sects indicated a despair in the world, typical of situations of a clash of different value-systems, which was often a concomitant of social superstratification and conquest, situations which actually prevailed in China prior to the T'ang time and during the Mongol period. Other messianic or quasi-messianic movements in China, which often revolved around Amitabha or Kuan-yin, indicated a belief in the unimportance of life on earth, especially the irrelevance of moral life. At least in popular belief, no repentence was necessary, only belief in grace.

Some of the Chinese messianic movements, to be sure, stressed the value of repentance,[15] but others concentrated entirely on the belief in salvation. None of them emphasized the concept of guilt. Religious systems such as these, in which the concept of grace is stressed, might be likened to absolutistic monarchism, because a supreme being can change the fate of an individual according to its own inclinations, whether or not that individual has committed sins in violation of divine laws and normally deserving punishment. Incidentally, the main difference between Chinese religions emphasizing grace and the original concept of grace in Christianity is that in Christian doctrine at least a feeling of guilt and usually acts of repentance are necessary conditions. The development of such a concept of grace as we find in Buddhist sects may well follow from the experience of bureaucratic absolutism in which it was not clear whether a good deed would receive worldly rewards or at least recognition, or whether a bad deed would receive punishment. It all depended upon the ruler and his administration. Perhaps the hedonistic attitudes which seem to be characteristic for at least some parts of T'ang literature and literati may be taken as indicating a similarly caused disinterest in sin and guilt: enjoy life today, as it is not certain what will come tomorrow.

After the diffusion of Buddhism into China, a "modern" folk religion developed which incorporated mainly Buddhist doctrines, some Taoist doctrines, and also beliefs of other, often local, origin. By the term "folk religion" we mean, from now on, the mainstream of this popular religion. In referring to those essentially Buddhist parts which represent simplified beliefs stemming from philosophical Buddhism, we may occasionally use the term folk Buddhism. Folk religion uses some of the philosophical scriptures of Buddhism (usually abbreviated versions of long texts) or original texts based upon such scriptures, as well as Taoist scriptures and texts of mixed character, often spiritualistic texts. While folk Buddhism as such was of great importance for the first time during the sixth to ninth centuries, and regained importance only in certain later periods, folk religion, at first without Buddhist elements, developed as a

---

[15] This found its expression in public confessions. Such confessions are known to be made by members of the "Taoist" sect of Chang Lu (Werner Eichhorn in *Deutsche Akademie d. Wissenschaften, Berlin, Inst. f. Orientforschung,* Vol. 3 [1955], No. 2, p. 322, n. 101), but were typical of Buddhist sects in T'ang time and earlier as well. It seems that such confessions were made in groups, on the basis of standardized texts or collections of sins, rather than individually and on the basis of the guilt feelings of the individual. But individual confessions are also reported in the literature. For instance, when there was a big storm, all persons on board a ship knelt down and "thought of their sins" (*Hsiao-tse chuan,* quoted in *T'ai-p'ing yü-lan,* 186, p. 7a-b).

continuous but changing stream from pre-Han time up to its present form.

This modern folk religion slowly developed a divine bureaucracy with a clear rank order, with divine ministries and divine red tape. It also developed the important concept of mutuality. A deity, although infinitely more powerful than man, still has certain obligations toward man, stemming from its office in the divine organization. A rain deity has a divine obligation to give rain for the benefit of man. It has the power to delay the rain, and may do so on the basis of its whims as well as a punishment for a sin committed by man. But if man feels free of any guilt, he may complain to the next-higher-ranking deity, and if the complaint is found to be justified, the rain deity can receive divine punishment, demotion, or even divine death. With these concepts, modern folk religion seems to correspond best to a system of bureaucratic contitutional monarchy.[16] And as in any such political system changes in the laws are possible and common, it was believed that changes in the divine laws also occurred.[17] Some laws, so people believed, were made more lenient,[18] but it also happened that a deity tightened or set up new laws if there seemed to be a necessity to do so.

This concept of change appears to be based, in part, on an originally Buddhist idea of change in human moral development. While in Judaism, Christianity, and Islam the character of man, and the divine institutions dealing with his merits and sins, have been unchangeable and everlasting from the beginning of the world to the last day, folk religion, probably ultimately based on the doctrine of *kalpa* (era, world period) in philosophical Buddhism, assumed that human beings were originally good, but had become bad as time went on, so that a system of punishments had to be set up. According to some popular texts no hells existed, because people were good up to the end of the Chou dynasty (around 250 B.C.). Only from then on did hells have to be created to punish the sinners.[19] The idea that the existing hells were no longer sufficient,

[16] According to folk beliefs in Yünnan, the underworld is thought of as a city with its city god and a part of a subterranean state with provincial judges (Francis L. K. Hsu, *Under the Ancestors Shadows* [New York, 1948], pp. 137–139). In a case which is believed to have happened in 1786, the judge in hell had to call interpreters because he had to deal with non-Chinese (*Yung-hsien-chai pi-chi*, 7, 3a).

[17] A Ming text reports that there are even amnesties in hell, at the same time that there are imperial amnesties on earth (*Wan-li yeh-huo pien*, 28, p. 715).

[18] The *Yü-li* which G. W. Clarke published (J/RAS, North China Branch, Vol. 28, No. 2, pp. 233ff.) has such clauses. Individual judges could be too lenient and then be demoted to deeper hells, such as Judge Pao (*T'ai-yang*, p. 3; Henry Doré, *Recherches sur les Superstitions en Chine* [Shanghai, 1911–1938], Vol. 6, pp. 167ff., hell five).

[19] *Tung-ming pao-chi*, chap. 9, p. 71.

because the number of sins and of sinners had increased so much in recent times, is found in the seventeenth century,[20] and strongly expressed in at least one twentieth century text.[21] Even other buildings, such as the "Hall of Wide Coldness" (*Kuang-han-tien*) in the moon, are not permanent or eternal. According to a text from the late eighteenth century,[22] it was built eight hundred years ago. The same book has another extremely significant story:

A certain Mr. Yang has by mistake been called into the netherworld. He is dismissed as soon as the mistake is clarified, but instead of immediately returning to the world, he meets an old friend, Mr. Yin, who invites him to visit a house of ill repute. Such an institution in the netherworld serves the needs of all the innumerable clerks and other employees. The girls in these houses are daughters or beloved concubines of covetous, greedy officials. The girls lose their social status in these houses; only age is important. Mr. Yang is quite appalled when he meets his bride in this establishment, but he uses the occasion and his rights as customer to spend the night with her. After a while, an order arrives that she be released and sent back to earth, because her father, who had been corrupt, had promised publicly to establish a welfare school in his district. Mr. Yang now also leaves the netherworld, visits his father-in-law, verifies the facts, marries his bride. In the bridal night, he asks her about their meeting in the other world. She seems not to remember anything, but she is not a virgin. The author of this story is apparently satisfied with this explanation of the loss of virginity, but he remarks that it was one of the bad laws of the earlier Chinese Ming dynasty to put innocent daughters and wives of criminals into state whorehouses, and he wonders why in the other world they still are continuing to apply a law which on the earth has already been outmoded for centuries.[23]

In some cases, the history of the development of hells poses problems to the Chinese scholar, as the following story indicates:

Mr. Ku died in 1874 but came back to life and reported about his visit in hell. He had met there a former friend and had asked him about the organization of hells. The friend told him that the prevailing system of ten hells corresponded to the system of the T'ang dynasty, in so far as each hell corresponded to one of the ten provinces of T'ang time. He also stated that before 1821 all officials in hell were men who had lived in the Ming time, that is, before 1644, while now all officials were men who had lived in the Manchu period, that is, after 1644. The author understands this statement to mean that even souls have no eternal life and die. Therefore, judges in hell have to be replaced from time to time as they die. But, he worries, the

[20] *Liao-chai chih-i,* Vol. 2, chap. 11, pp. 199–203. A drama of the late Ming period, *Nü-hung sha* (*Ch'ü-hai,* I, 431–433) also speaks of the plan to build new hells to punish corrupt examination officials. It should be mentioned that texts also mention new building activities in the heavenly regions (for instance, the Ming drama *Hsiu-wen chi* [*Ch'ü-hai,* I, 320–322]).

[21] *Tung-ming pao-chi,* chap. 9, p. 71.

[22] *Hsieh-to,* 10, 7a.

[23] *Ibid.,* 6, 7b.

system of ten provinces was in use only during a brief part of the T'ang dynasty and came to an end already in 732. Why did they not change the organization in hell since then? [24]

Folk religion incorporates in these beliefs in the change of divine laws the Indian Buddhist belief in deterioration of mankind during the duration of a *kalpa*—a deterioration which leads to the total destruction of a wicked mankind and to a new *kalpa* in which, at the beginning, all men are good. Folk religion also incorporates here the belief of Confucian philosophers that conditions in society were excellent at the time of China's earliest rulers, but tended to deteriorate from generation to generation in later times, with no clear doctrine as to how this situation could be remedied except by following Confucian rules.

We should add here that a much weaker undercurrent of Confucian philosophy believed in upward evolution, in moral improvement of society. As there seems to be some correlation between a youth-centered culture and belief in moral progress, as against an age-centered society and belief in moral deterioration, we should expect the latter belief to be dominant in a society which from its beginnings was extremely age-centered.

[24] *Erh-ju*, I, 12b–13a.

CHAPTER TWO

The Various Hells: Their Structure, Population, and Administration

Description

Buddhism had already in India developed the concept of numerous hells in which criminals are punished for different types of crime. Chinese Buddhism shows two lines of thought: a belief in eighteen (or sixteen) hells and a belief in eight (or ten) hells.[1] Both systems seem to have a common root. In the system of eighteen hells, we find eight hot hells and eight cold hells. Either between these two sets or after the eight cold hells are two other special places of punishment or of judgment. The system of eight (or ten) hells has only the eight hot hells, introduced by an initial place of judgment and followed by a final place of judgment. Buddhist schools differed here, but we do not want to go further into doctrinal points. We only want to point out that the Tibetans [2] and Mongols [3] seem to have believed more in the idea of cold hells,[4] while the Chinese seem to have developed mostly the idea of hot hells, because, perhaps, exposure to cold was well known to Tibetans and Mongols and as much dreaded by them as exposure to extreme heat

[1] A Sung text (*Kui-hua*, 4, 3b) mentions that the hells are under Yama and that the *Āgama* scriptures mentioned eighteen hells. It was unknown since when the concept of ten hells became known.

[2] Robert Ekvall, University of Washington, Seattle, was kind enough to ask his Tibetan informant, Dezhung Rinpoche, about the present-day Tibetan concepts of hells. His list and description are very close to the early Indian-Chinese texts.

[3] Walther Heissig, *Helden-, Höllenfahrts- und Schelmengeschichten der Mongolen* (Berlin, 1962), published a Mongolian text composed around 1700 and preserved in the Royal Library, Copenhagen, No. 418. This text has eighteen hells.

[4] Samuel Beal, *A Catena of Buddhist Scriptures from the Chinese* (London, 1871), pp. 57ff., also has the eighteen hells and brings the Indian names of these hells together with their names in Chinese.

was by the Chinese. Interestingly enough, the descriptions which I was able to collect of the cold hells all show a great lack of imagination— after all, if a place is extremely cold, there is not much variation in grades and shades conceivable. Moreover, the descriptions of the sins for which a person is sent to one of the cold hells are also much briefer and show less imagination than the description of the sins which bring a person into the hot hells. The system of hot hells in Chinese popular thought also has some cold spots, but these are not special hells, only small places within a hell. One gains the impression that the fear of freezing has impressed the Tibetans and Mongols more than the Chinese. The eight hot hells of Chinese folk religion all have specific names that go back to Chinese Buddhist tradition of, at the latest, the sixth century A.D., and these names are translations or transliterations of Indian names. Some popular texts occasionally mix up names or sequences, but the general line remained the same from 500 to 1960 A.D. As we are mainly interested in the present time, we shall not discuss all texts which are known, but shall use a twentieth century text as our basic text, from which we shall refer backward to earlier texts as far as this is desirable. As already mentioned, Buddhist texts as early as the second century A.D. have the concept of hells and mention crimes for which one is sent to these hells. The text of the sixth century, the *Cheng-fa nien-ch'u ching*,[5] is the first text which described the hells and the sins in great detail. Tun-huang texts of the time before 1000 A.D. normally incorporate descriptions of hells and sins into the story of the saint Mu-lien,[6] which was very popular and still is known to many Chinese. It seems that before 1400 a number of books appeared which enumerated sins and meritorious deeds with a kind of merit and demerit point system; such books represented a different trend of tradition.[7] Between 1400 and 1600 many books were published in which people were admonished to better themselves, the *shan-shu*. The most famous book of this type is the "imperial edict" (*sheng-yü*), an admonition of the

[5] This text is published in the *Taishô Tripitaka*, Vol. 17, pp. 27ff. It is said to be translated by Chü T'an during the time of the T'o-pa dynasty. The text in its present form has an obvious break after sub-hell seven of hell number one (p. 29b) and some disorder in the discussions of hells two and three, but it seems to be in better condition later. A text from the fifth century (*Taishô Tripitaka*, Vol. 16, p. 83b) mentions only ten hells.

[6] The story of Mu-lien (Maudgalyāyana) is reported by Wilhelm Grube, *Pekinger Volkskunde*, p. 56, and others. It is found in the *T'ai-p'ing kuang-chi*, chap. 251, and in Tun-huang fragments, published in *Tun-huang pien-wen chi*, 6, p. 701. *Tun-huang pien-wen-chi*, 6, pp. 714ff., a manuscript from 921 A.D., describes only five hells, and not in detail. The Mongol text (see n. 3 above) is also a Mu-lien story. The seventeenth century drama *Lung-hua hui* (*Ch'ü-hai*, I, 481–485) is a variant of the Mu-lien story and also contains a description of the various hells.

[7] See Robert van Gulik, *Sexual Life in Ancient China* (Leiden, 1961), pp. 246ff.

emperor to all classes of people to be good and to follow the law, issued at various times by various emperors. Similarly, between 1400 and 1600, leading personalities issued books of moralistic character with the openly declared aim of improving the moral character of the lower classes.[8] We might add that these books began to proliferate in those centuries in which—according to other texts—crimes by juveniles and by urban gangs had been on the increase. The correlation between increase of moralistic books and increase of crime seems clear, but our general knowledge of the tie is still so incomplete that at this moment nothing more definite can be said. Here seems to be a fertile field for further research, especially in the possible connections between quick urbanization and increase of urban crime in Central China, as early as about 500 years ago.

Shan-shu of various kinds have been printed again and again up to the present time. They very often consist of a main text, to which commentaries and case reports are often added. Perhaps the most widely read *shan-shu* of the eighteenth century is the *T'ai-shang kan-ying-p'ien.* It is claimed that the standard text was written even before the eleventh century. The version which is now most widely accepted, an edition of 1749, contains a long commentary to every sentence, in which, by means of quotations from Confucian texts, the editor wanted to prove that this book was in complete agreement with the teaching of Confucius. But at the same time, other texts were published, sometimes under other names, such as *T'ai-shang pao-fa t'u-shuo,* which added a different, less philosophical, commentary to each sentence, followed by one long and sometimes one or more brief case reports. The case reports illustrated the consequences of good or bad actions by telling what happened to a man who did a good or a bad deed. Each such section is preceded by a picture which illustrates the first case report, and by one or several poems on the case.[9] It may be significant that the book has had approximately thirty stories about the consequences of good deeds, but over 160 about bad actions.[10] The *T'ai-shang pao-fa t'u-shuo* shows very well how books of this type continuously changed their form. Its 1694 editor mentions that he re-edited an older text and that he added new stories. But some stories in the book refer to the eighteenth

---

[8] Much to the dismay of the writers of such books, scholars usually took a dim view of them. A scholar who heard somebody reciting the *T'ai-shang kan-ying ching* when he strolled through a temple in Hangchow, said: "This kind of book is only good to trick stupid men and stupid women. How can educated persons recite it?" (*T'ai-shang pao-fa t'u-shuo,* 4, p. 25b).

[9] This book was made available to me by the kindness of Professor Paul Serruys, who bought the 1903 edition in Peking.

[10] *T'ai-shang pao-fa t'u-shuo,* p. 15a.

century and, therefore, must have been added by the 1755 editor. This man, Huang Cheng-yüan, said, "As the heart of man is bored by the old things and as man likes the new things . . . I followed the footsteps of Hsü Hao-sha [the supposed author of the text] but took my examples mainly from new reports." [11] He wanted the book so simple that even women and children could read it easily and would find it as interesting as short stories.[12] The printing of such books is meritorious. The texts are often deposited in temples, and every visitor can pick up and keep a copy. This custom spread even into California. I picked up a book of this type, printed in Canton in 1905 after an edition of 1869, the *T'ai-yang/yin chen-ching* (The True Book of Sun and Moon) in the ruins of a Chinese temple in Napa, California.[13] It contains a brief incantation to the sun and to the moon, followed by four short stories on how the recitation and printing of this text had brought good luck to the believers. Again, each sentence of the incantation has a commentary which stresses three points: do not stay in foreign countries too long, send money back home, and (for women) do not get angry if the amounts sent should be small. This clearly indicates that the book was specially adapted for distribution among Chinese in foreign countries.

Although books like this and the *T'ai-shang pao-fa t'u-shuo* are clearly written for the less educated, we know that many highly educated men in the later years liked to read the more sophisticated editions, such as the *T'ai-shang kan-ying-p'ien*. In the middle of the nineteenth century, the book *Yü-li* gained great popularity among the less educated. It also has been published in many different editions [14] and contains pictures of the different hells and punishments, together with a text

[11] *Ibid.,* p. 12a.

[12] *Ibid.,* p. 12b.

[13] Visit on January 20, 1963. The temple was devoted to the Pei-chi ("God of the North Pole"), as was the temple in Marysville, California. The shrine is now stored in a second-floor room of a former Chinese drugstore in the area which once was Napa's Chinatown.

[14] The *Yü-li* which I used as my main text in the following discussions is a modern Taiwan print of a 1928 edition. It contains an 1855 preface and earlier prefaces from 1809 and 1810. Very similar, but not completely so, is a print also from the time before 1930 with a preface of 1858. The pictures in both texts are made from the same type of plates. Henry Doré, *Recherches sur les Superstitions en Chine* (Shanghai, 1911–1938), Vol. 6, pp. 167–196, gives excerpts and some pictures from another *Yü-li*. The text seems to have been quite similar, but the pictures of Doré deviate strongly and are made in a different style. It has been remarked already by others that Doré's illustrations are open to serious doubts as to their authenticity. Finally, G. W. Clarke, "The Yü-li, or Precious Records," in the *Journal of the Royal Asiatic Society, China Branch*, Vol. 28, No. 2, pp. 233–400, published a text printed in 1857 with illustrations which are quite similar in content, but are primitive woodcuts and not yet modern lithographs as in the editions mentioned above. Clarke's text states that the text was composed before the year 1000 A.D. and the first edition was dated 1031.

which does not always follow the pictures closely. The *Yü-li* is mentioned in other *shan-shu* as a kind of basic text, for instance in the *Hsing-shan fu-pao p'ien,* printed in Szu-ch'uan after 1875 and reporting a visit to the different hells made by a Mr. Li Ch'ang-ch'ing, who was killed in 1862 in Han-chung where he was an educational officer. Li was later revived and reported his impressions. His description of the hells differs in details from that of the *Yü-li* and the *Tung-ming pao-chi,* which we will discuss later, but in general follows the same system. Mr. Li saw in hell number seven special iron beds for opium smokers who smoked red-hot pipes, and he asked what would happen to people who come to opium innocently or find themselves in a situation in which they could not refuse opium. The judge said that they should read the *Yü-li,* in which they would find out how their guilt could be redeemed.

The *Yü-li* is also regarded as one of the *shan-shu.*[15] I picked up a copy of a recent print of the *Yü-li* in a Taiwanese temple, where it had been deposited for the benefit of the visitors who could and should pick them up and read them, and severe punishments were indicated for persons who might destroy or deface such books.

Our main text is another such *shan-shu,* the *Tung-ming pao-chi.* This book I found also in a Taiwanese temple. I chose it for demonstration because it has the most details of all the books at my disposal, and is of the most recent date. It is written in the style of a popular novel.[16] The main part describes how different visitors are allowed to inspect the different hells in order to be able to report to human beings about the

[15] On the history, development, and importance of these books, see T. Sakai, *Studies of Chinese shan-shu, Popular Books on Morality* (Tokyo, 1960).

[16] We have the impression that many of these descriptions of hells are the result of shamanistic or spiritualistic sessions. Chao Wei-pang, in *Folklore Studies,* Vol. 3 (1944), describes such a session in which a part of the hells is mentioned. Two modern Taiwanese descriptions are in the form of a seven-word epic poem in Fukien dialect. Both have some general similarity with the Mu-lien story, and one text could be called a *shan-shu.* This text, *Tseng Erh-niang shao hao-hsiang ko,* has two sisters, one pious, one sinful. One day, both die and are brought into hell. Here the sinner is saved from the worst punishments by the good sister, and both go through all ten hells, seeing the tortures which sinners have to suffer. Finally, the earth god brings both sisters back to life. The sinner is now reformed and becomes pious. The other text, *Lo-yin hsiang-pao hsin-ko,* clearly mentions a shamanistic session. Here a young husband falls ill. In spite of all attempts he dies, but before his death he asks his wife to call all his relatives so that they see him die and do not believe that she murdered him. She is so frightened that she does not go to his relatives, and his brother, indeed, is planning to accuse her of murder. She calls a shamanistic helper and passes into hell. She sees all the hells, whose descriptions differ from those in other texts, and has difficulty in finding her husband, as she cannot read the lists of the hell population because she is illiterate. Finally somebody helps her, she finds her man and brings him back with great trouble and with the help of the earth god, so that he comes to life again.

horrible punishments which sinners have to expect. Our visitors are
often not too much interested in the detail and have many hells only
described to them, while they take a look at others which they regard as
more interesting. Often, they laugh when they see the most terrible
tortures because the convulsions of the sinners seem funny to them. Or
they lecture to sinners who beg them to ask the judges for mercy because
they cannot bear the tortures any more. The edition of this rather crude
book which I have used must have been composed around 1935, because it contains references to political events which happened after the
First World War, but evidently no events of the Second World War.[17]
It refers often to persons and places in Erh-yüan, a district in northwes-
tern Yünnan province, and seems to have special connections with this
area of China, but apart from the novelistic embellishments of the text, it
follows very closely the tradition of books such as the *Yü-li*. However,
the *Tung-ming pao-chi* shows a strong influence of spiritualism; for
example, deities are called by the spirit tablet; they answer via the
tablet.[18] On the other hand, the *Yü-li* indicates that it was written by a
man who, after failure in the examinations, became a businessman, and
who had success in business because of composing the book.[19] The
Tung-ming pao-chi does not show a similar connection with business,
although, like all such books, it certainly addresses itself to the middle
and lower classes. Let me give a kind of analytic view of the relevant
parts of the book.

During his lifetime, a human being is responsible for his actions, with
some exceptions. In some cases, as a consequence of the actions of a
man, either his wife or children may die, or they may suffer a horrible
fate, not as a consequence of their own deeds, but as a way of punishing
the criminal man.[20] In fact, they may not have committed any sin (either
in this or in a previous life) which would justify such punishment; it is
purely the result of the father's or husband's deeds. From my experience,
cases in which a whole clan was said to be punished in such a way for a
crime committed by one clan member are extremely rare; the sufferers
are the closest relatives only. Otherwise, a man (or a woman) receives
punishment for his (or her) own actions in a previous life, in the form of
a rebirth in a low-class family, or—even worse—in a low-class family
among a barbarian tribe; or the individual is reborn with physical or
psychical defects, or dies at an early age, or suffers for many years. If

[17] My text was a very coarse, new print, on rough paper, without date, in two
volumes.
[18] On spiritualism in China in general, see Alan J. Elliott, *Chinese Spirit-
Medium Cults in Singapore* (London, 1955), with references.
[19] *Yü-li*, p. 10.
[20] *Ibid.*, p. 6.

people—in spite of such handicaps as they may have to start with—commit good deeds, the outlook for the coming rebirth is good. If they commit crimes, they may receive immediate punishment by the human agencies, usually by the courts. But whether or not a culprit is caught and punished by human justice, thirty-eight thousand heavenly officials watch all humans during the day, and thirty-eight thousand others watch during the night. These officials are divided into three categories: the gods of the hearth, the spirits passing through the air, and the spirits of the rain gutter. They see or hear whatever is done inside the house or outside, take careful note, and report to the office of the Tung-yüeh god (God of the Eastern Peak). Here, thirty-six hundred officials compose a monthly report to the Ta-ti (Great Ruler). At the end of each year, a final report is made in three copies; one copy goes to the Jade Emperor (Yü Huang-ti), one to the ten hells, and one to the three officials who mete out the fate.[21] Thus, every bad act, but also every good act, of every person is known and recorded.

A punishment received on earth is only a part of the punishment to be received by the personal soul. After death, the personal soul is brought to the office of the local city god (Ch'eng-huang). Persons who have acted morally will sit in nice rooms; but sinners will receive a preliminary punishment and then either fall into the Blood River and drift into the first hell, or walk naked and dirty on a slippery road, cross the "border between this and the other world," and pass through the remaining stations called "the spirit gate," "the mountains where one thinks of the home," the icy "mountains of the lonely rest," the "cliff of the breaking of money," where all money which relatives put into the coffin or burned for the dead will be destroyed and useless, and the "waterfall of fright," where the worst sinners drown and are eaten by fish. There is a "love river," which has its origin in the "sea of sexual thoughts" and which brings together all the dirt of the world. Sinning women drift in this river to the "sea of punishment." Thus, sinners arrive by different ways in the first hell, while good persons walk in comfort along another road to the place of rebirth (hell number ten).[22]

The first hell has no counterpart in the old text of the sixth century. It is a kind of receiving station whose main item is a mirror in which, objectively, all sins committed by a person are visible. From here on, all differences of status, class, age, or sex cease to exist; everybody is treated according to the same standards. The pictures in the mirror indicate the punishments which the sinners will have to endure. Sinners are here assigned to different places on the basis of a verdict in a trial. Thus,

21 *Tung-ming pao-chi,* chap. 23.
22 *Ibid.,* chaps. 5–8.

popular belief has two places of judgment: the hall of the city god and the first hell. All persons who appear for judgment are not necessarily dead; we have many stories, often quite humorous, of living people who request a trial or are called for a trial. As such stories, which are innumerable in Chinese literature, provide illuminating details of our description of hells, we will give some examples.

One day, a child picks some flowers in a deserted graveyard. Inadvertently, he falls into an old coffin, is frightened, and falls very ill as soon as he is home again. Out of his mouth speaks a geomancer who asks his life as punishment for the desecration of his coffin. Mr. Wang, the father of the child, prays for mercy, but the prayer has no success, whereupon Mr. Wang goes into the city god temple and sleeps in it. During his sleep, his soul is called to the trial of his son, with the geomancer as plaintiff. The city god acquits the child and punishes the geomancer; a good geomancer would certainly find a place where his own coffin would be safe. If he was unable to secure his own coffin, he must have cheated many people during his lifetime. His punishment—given long after his death—is to be devoured by hungry dogs in a special netherworld department. The next day, the child is well again. It is seen that the bones of the geomancer have been eaten by dogs.[23]

Interesting in this story is the assumption of the dead geomancer—a spirit himself—that even an unintended act of a small child deserves harsh punishment, and the trial in which a dead spirit accuses a still-living child.

In another, humorous, story we find a beggar complaining to the god of this hell, that he has been treated unfairly.

The rich have fine food, fine dress and beautiful women, while he has nothing of all this. The god, thereupon, gives him a better tongue, a better body, and strong sex organs. When he comes back to life the next morning, he is unwilling to eat his simple food; he does not want to dress in his beggar's dress, nor does he even look at his wife. Whereupon she remarks: "You just forgot to ask for the only really important thing: money." [24]

This motif of complaint with the god of hell by the technique of sleeping in the temple is very common and shows the belief that juridical errors might occur even in hell and that redress is possible.

While the main purpose of this first hell is the determination of punishment, three categories of sinners already receive punishment here in the three special subdepartments of this hell. There is the prison for Buddhist monks and for Confucians. It is for monks who violated the basic rules of Buddhism and for Confucians who talked about Confucian moral canons while violating them, or accepted heterodox doctrines, criticized philosophers of the old time as reactionary persons, got inter-

[23] *Hsieh-to,* 9, 4a–b.
[24] *Ibid.,* 5, 4b.

ested in Western history and teachings, or composed erotic poetry, painted erotic paintings, and thus corrupted chaste girls and innocent children. There is the "factory of hunger and thirst" in which there are persons who thoughtlessly or without a valid reason committed suicide. They suffer here for months or years and then are brought back to the scene of their suicide. Here, they again suffer hunger and thirst, as they are not allowed to eat the sacrifices. But if they behave and do not appear to frighten people or induce other people to serve as their replacement by inducing them to commit suicide, they return to hell number one and receive only the punishments for their remaining sins. In this "factory" there are mainly women, we are told in the book. Finally, there is a "place for mending the classics" in which we find people who cheated during religious festivals, who when reading holy texts looked at women, who used their money for flirting or gambling instead of for religious works. The "place" is a set of low, dark houses with tiny lamps, in which the sinners recite books which they can hardly read in the darkness, and in which they mend books.

Hell number two corresponds to the hell number one of the old text of the sixth century. The main place is the "living big prison" for people who had been warned some time before their crimes were detected by worldly justice, to see whether they would repent. After they have been found out and executed by worldly justice, they come to this hell for further punishment. Here we find also persons whose bodies are still alive though their souls are already in hell: the mentally sick, the cripples, and the very sick. Their souls are already tortured while their bodies still are kept alive by the body soul. A story of humorous character may illustrate this concept:

> The god brought a father-and-son team of successful lawyers down for a trial and asked them why they did not take an honest job, such as farmer or merchant. The lawyers answered that people, by giving them money, obliged them to take their cases. They really had no other choice. The god decided to stop them; he blinded the father and cut off the son's arms. Indeed, soon after this "dream," both became cripples, but the father continued to dictate defense letters to his son, who wrote them with his toes.[25]

There are sixteen sub-hells in this hell, with punishment for sexual crimes, bad family relations, cheating or robbing other people, or incompetent actions by doctors, geomancers, or astrologers. One of these sixteen sub-hells is icy, a punishment for sons who had warm clothing but let their parents freeze.

Each following hell now is regarded as being more severe than the

---

[25] *Ibid.*, 6a–b.

earlier ones. In each of them, therefore, we find persons who committed crimes worse than those punished in the earlier hells. But some crimes are so bad that sinners receive punishment in all hells, one after the other. For other crimes a special system of transfers is developed. Thus, for instance, a sinner may first be punished by hell three, sub-hell seven, and then is transferred to hell four, sub-hell nine, and so forth.

Hell three, called the black-rope hell like its first sub-hell, contains largely sinners who violated rules of social behavior, who sinned against the state or the community, that is, who violated basic Confucian principles, including rules of the family. To give an impression of the character of the sub-hells and the sins, I shall give a summary of the sixteen sub-hells of this hell number three. There is first the black-rope sub-hell, in which the sinners are tied together and choked to death. Afterward they are revived with a fan, and the treatment begins again. This is punishment for violation of the five basic Confucian rules. There are many officials and many women in this hell. The officials did not serve the state faithfully, wanting only to become wealthy. Others paid attention to Western teachings and did not care about Confucian rules. The women imitated the actions of men, wanted women's rights, did not keep the rules of the harem, did not honor their husbands or in-laws, or got a divorce from their husbands. Here are also sons who strolled around and enjoyed their lives in faraway places while their parents waited for them day and night, until they died of grief.

Sub-hell number two is the "salt prison," in which people are pickled in a salt lake. Such people secretly did harm to others without letting them know about it.

Sub-hell number three is the "hemp rope and cangue prison" for the same crimes as sub-hell number one. Then follows number four, the "piercing-of-bones hell," in which people are hanged on hooks, and iron dogs come to eat them. Similar is number five, the "meat distribution hell." People in these two hells had been adopted legally into other families, but had returned, after marriage, to the families of their birth, so that their adoptive parents did not receive ancestral sacrifices.

In the "shaving prison" (number six) the faces are cut off from persons who did not care about honesty and moral cleanliness, persons who were not loyal, women who were not chaste, robbers, immoral persons, and men who spread false doctrines.

The "fat-cutting prison" (number seven) is a place of treatment for greedy officials, office servants, cheating merchants, stealing soldiers. Here are people who sold with false weights. They go to sub-hells numbers eight and nine, then to hell number four, sub-hell nine.

In the "skinning prison" (number eight) persons are skinned and

The Second Hell. Woodcut, late nineteenth century. (*From* Journal of the China Branch of the Royal Asiatic Society, *1897, plate 10*)

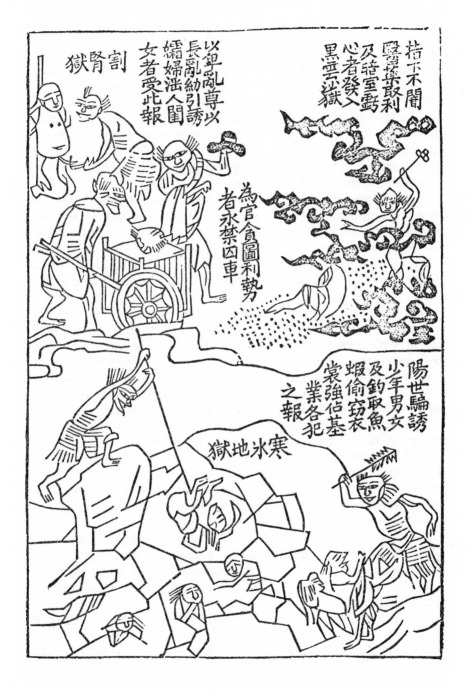

The Second Hell. Woodcut, late nineteenth century. (From Journal of the China Branch of the Royal Asiatic Society, *1897, plate 11*)

their skin is given to snakes and dogs. Here we find mainly officials who cut off people's land and took it away from them.

In the "blood-drinking hell" (number nine) persons who exploited the sweat and work of others have their blood sucked out by worms.

The "liver-excising hell" (number ten) is for persons who were jealous when others had success and happy when they failed; for women who became jealous when their husbands took a concubine and had a child by her; for people who destroyed tombs, exchanged corpses in order to occupy an auspicious tomb, or for people who did not take care of the tombs of their family.

The "eye-gouging prison" (number eleven), in which the eyes are taken out and eaten by dogs and birds, is for a variety of sinners: persons who did not honor printed paper, stepped on it or destroyed it; who did not honor their superiors; who flirted or looked into the harems of others; who loved to start law suits, made denunciations, wrote divorce letters, falsified contracts, changed seals or data on debt certificates.

The "foot-cutting prison" (number twelve) is for soldiers who ran away in war with their equipment; for persons who, being slaves, stole their master's money and ran away; for persons who embezzled their boss's money and opened a shop in another place, causing bankruptcy of their former boss. Here are soldiers who caused punishment of their commander because they fled in a battle; men who defaulted on a debt and thus involved the guarantors of their debt; finally, women who thought that their husbands were ugly or poor, who flirted with other men, committed adultery, and finally ran away with their lovers.

The "small prison for pulling out finger and toe nails and the breaking of kneecaps" (number thirteen) offers different punishments for the same crimes as sub-hell number twelve. Similarly, the "prison in which one is hung upside down" (number fourteen) punishes the same crimes as sub-hell number one.

The "frog prison" (number fifteen) is dark, and people are bitten by ugly worms, frogs, snakes, scorpions, centipedes, in the nose, ears, mouth, or eyes. Here we find people who secretly did harm to others, as in sub-hell one, who broke up marriages, broke up families, divided friends and relatives.

Finally, in the "prison for taking out the heart" (sub-hell sixteen of hell three), the heart is taken out and its condition is analyzed.

Sinners who committed still worse crimes are found in hell four, the "hell of united greatness" (ho-ta). Here again we find a variety of crimes and of punishments. Most of the crimes are asocial acts: theft of bricks which were serving as a pavement, theft of parts of bridges or of street lamps, putting garbage on the roads. Other cases of theft: farmers who stole grain from other farmers' fields, took their pigs, or cut their trees; scholars who stole writing brushes, books, ink, or rubbings; craftsmen who stole implements. Then, we have here crimes connected with the business world: embezzlement of trust funds, use of false weights, charging of exorbitant interest rates, selling of wet rice or of fake medicines, paying with false money. Men who made promises and broke them later are here, as well as persons who spread rumors about the harem affairs of others or who talked against the holy books. We find here also quack doctors and practitioners of witchcraft, producers of love potions. They are together with persons who liked to eat beef and dog meat, who gave impure gifts as sacrifices or fed others with unclean food. Geomancers are here who destroyed the burial grounds of others to have their own dead buried there. Finally, people who let their parents suffer need while they are rich come to this hell; people who are lazy in the service of their parents, who waste money in gambling and whoring while their parents suffer, who criticize their parents, who waste all their property after their parent's death, and brothers who cheat one another when they divide the parental property among themselves.

The fifth hell, called *sen-lo* hell, has many outstanding properties. When a person dies, he sees on his way to the hells his own body at home and remembers his life. But when he comes to hell number five, he passes the "looking-at-the-home terrace" (*Wang-hsiang-t'ai*). By now, the body is decayed and the soul becomes aware that return is no longer possible. The soul also sees how the family by now has changed into a new form, perhaps has more or less forgotten the dead and rearranged its life. In this melancholy mood, the soul comes to the main office and faces the most famous of all judges, Yen-lo wang (King Yama of Indian texts), the one judge who is known to everybody. The crimes that bring the soul into this place are mainly crimes against Buddhist religion: murder of humans, killing of animals, slander of deities. But even more important, and closely related to these violations, are sexual crimes. In fact "immorality is the greatest crime; it cannot be pardoned." [26] The immorality consists of incest with wives of brothers, or with father's concubines, or of incest of fathers with their son's wives. Such sinners are punished all through hells numbers one to nine. Then they are reborn in the form of an animal or a bird and have no chance ever to be reborn as human beings. But worse still, their wives, children, and grandchildren are also punished, and all of these will die. Thus even the ancestors of such sinners are punished because they have nobody left

[26] *Tung-ming pao-chi,* chap. 15, p. 174.

who will perform the ancestral sacrifices for them, and they will remain forever hungry.

Now, in this hell, five new sub-hells have recently been created in addition to the older sub-hells which were established much earlier. The new hells are specifically for persons who had contacts with foreigners: "The worst is in the present time to have contacts with foreigners or to buy machines and arms" [27] and to copy foreign traits. The fictional visitors to these sub-hells saw persons in Western dress, with eyeglasses and official headgear. Women were dressed in Japanese or European clothes that were tight and short. Sometimes they had their hair cut short. One of the sub-hells is like a theater, but the performance consists of administering punishments on the stage. Another section is like a dance hall, but people dance on red-hot iron boards. There is an amusement pavilion like those in the big cities, with women painted and made-up all over, and waitresses who offer beer, foreign drinks, wine, cigars, and cigarettes; but the drinks are in reality liquid copper or iron, the cookies are iron balls, the cigarettes burn the smokers. Another sub-hell is full of weapons, including smokeless cannons from Germany, machine guns, airplanes, balloons, torpedo boats, but also old, traditional Chinese weapons. The visitors saw an air show where the aircraft is stopped in midair and crashes. Poisonous gas is applied to the sinners. Although warfare had developed in China prior to contact with the West, we read, the Westerners put all their ingenuity into this field and made daily new and more horrible weapons. Now, by using electricity, they have taken nature's secrets and their only grief is that they still are not able to destroy all mankind.[28] But a more terrible war will certainly come.

Two new sub-hells are for persons who concoct aphrodisiacs by using parts of human fetuses or of pregnant women; who engage in perverted sexual practices; who practice magic, especially such types of magic in which the soul of a murdered child is used as a slave of the murderer. In this sub-hell, we find the adherents of unorthodox secret religions or secret organizations, many of which used such and other magic tricks.

Finally, there is a new sub-hell, created between 1851 and 1861, for persons who believe in such false religions as those that claim that the soul ascends to heaven, and who turned against Chinese religions and ancestor worship. Some of them have used such false doctrines when they were involved in criminal suits and tried to win their suits by international intervention. These persons—obviously Christians—are still Chinese and remain under the jurisdiction of Chinese deities, what-

[27] *Ibid.,* p. 180.
[28] *Ibid.,* p. 190.

ever their own religion may tell them. Therefore, after death, they will
be sent to punishment in the hells. If their crimes were only relatively
light, they will be reborn as slaves, beggars, or paupers in a foreign
country; but if the crimes were severe, they will be reborn as cows,
horses, or other animals in a foreign country. Because they had turned
their hearts to foreign countries, they will not be allowed to return to
China.[29]

Hell six is the "hell of the great crying"; hell five is often called the
"hell of crying," because it is relatively less severe than the sixth Hell. In
this hell we find many sinners who have been punished before but who
complained about their sentence. Their cases are studied once again,
their guilt is once again established and, thereupon, they receive added
punishments because they still do not show insight and repentance.
Crimes punished here are those against deities and Buddha and the basic
Buddhist laws, as well as crimes against the basic Confucian laws concerning the family. But we also find here many political criminals:
ministers who murdered their rulers; rebels, bandits, and robbers;
officials who tortured prisoners more than necessary; generals who permitted plundering and wilful murder by soldiers.

Hell seven is the "hot hell" in which we find very many "transfers"
from earlier hells. The sinners starting out here are those receiving
punishment for violations of the Confucian rules concerning service to
parents, and friendship. Then we have another group of sinners who in
spite of their unclean condition went into temples. These men had used
human fetuses and other aphrodisiacs in order to prolong their life.
Many women are found in this place: women who mistreated their
servants; women who caused the death of others because of their loose
talk or calumnies; women who induced their husbands to cheat or to
mistreat the parents of the husband or to insist upon division of the
family property. The main feature in this hell is the oil kettle in which
practically all persons end who committed severe sins.

Hell eight is the "superlative hot hell," again for crimes against the
rules of Confucianism, for bandits, and for special types of sex crimes.
For instance, here are persons who operated whorehouses in the big
cities, persons who bought the daughters of poor people to use them as
whores and often mistreated and exploited these unfortunate girls so
much that they committed suicide. The special feature in this place is the
two *nai-ho* bridges—one for sinners and the other for good people. Rain-
bow-like, the bridges cross over a dirty, muddy river with copper snakes
and iron fish that attack all sinners who fall down from the sinner's

[29] *Ibid.,* pp. 203–204.

bridge, which has no railing and is only a few inches broad. The good people, after crossing the other, comfortable bridge, reach the tenth hell directly.

Hell nine, called the *A-pi* (Avitchi) hell, is twice as large as all the others. Here we find writers of erotic literature, painters of erotic scenes, producers of sexual instruments, together with persons who committed crimes against the state, killers of animals, thieves, murderers, and people who did not serve their parents well. This hell is the last of the punitive hells.

After "treatment," which may take a long time, the souls are brought into the tenth hell. The main installation in this hell is the "wheel of rebirths." Nearby is a building with 365 stories overlooking all parts of the world. Here are eight main offices.

In the first office, officials check whether the files of the arriving souls are complete and correct. If not, they are sent back to the earlier hells. If the files are in order, a second office adjudicates the conditions for the next life. Good souls are destined to be reborn in situations where they will become lower or higher officials. Other good souls get their reward indirectly by honors that their sons, parents, or husbands will receive or have received.

The third office deals with persons who have not been very good. According to their deeds in the earlier life, they may be sent into a life in which they have much work but little income; or they may even be poor, hungry, blind, deaf, or ill during all of their next life. Very bad criminals will become animals.

The fourth office checks whether the individual, during his lifetime on earth, had received a good deed from someone and whether he had returned this kindness; similarly, whether unjust suffering had already been balanced by revenge. If not, repayment and balancing of such accounts is arranged. For instance, if A was bad to B in their previous lives, so that B died of grief, in the next life B might become A's son and waste all of A's wealth and cause much grief to A.

The fifth office determines the length of the next life. The "classical" difficulty bothering the author of the book is that long life does not correlate with wealth, or with good or bad actions, in that, for example, some persons are murdered although they had committed no sin which could explain this fate.

The sixth office determines the future marriage: for instance, if, during the previous life, Mr. A treated Mr. B well, but B was unable before his death to repay this good deed, Mr. B might become Mr. A's wife in the next life, in order to repay him by being a good wife. In this office, also, future intelligence is determined.

In the seventh office special cases are studied and adjusted. For instance, there are souls who acted so badly in their previous lives that they would never be reborn as humans; there are people who had been committed to a very poor life, yet they had tried to do many good works in spite of their adverse fate; there were souls who had previously lived in the body of an animal but who had received a special order from the Jade Emperor (Yü Huang-ti). Finally, there were souls whose cases underwent special investigation, whereupon conversion of punishment was recommended.

Then the souls come to the eighth office, in which they are given symbols indicating their future form in life. They may be given horns, feathers, scales, ploughs, axes, or garments of high officials. In a story from the end of the eighteenth century this is nicely illustrated:

> Mr. Chao, known as a good scholar, is complaining about his physical ugliness. He comes into the netherworld, where in an office, obviously our eighth office, he meets an old friend, a well-known painter. This man has been given the job to paint the faces of people on the basis of two books which contain the models. The system is that poor people receive good faces, while people of high rank receive ugly faces. The poor need good looks, for they have nothing else. Chao tries, by adducing cases from history, to disprove this theory. Finally, the painter touches up his face a bit. When awake, Mr. Chao looks better, but his intelligence has suffered so that he never passes his examinations.[30]

With their symbols, the souls go to "Mother Meng," a kind of amusement park in which many waitresses under the direction of an old woman offer drinks in a number of tents. This drink, which everybody is forced to drink, is the drink of forgetting the entire past. Now, they are sent over one of six bridges leading to eighteen thousand roads. Each road leads to some part of the world and to some form of rebirth.

But this "administrative" activity is not yet all there is in the tenth hell. There is also "hellish" activity, since it contains the "iron circle" for long-term punishments.[31] Over a period of up to a thousand years, people receive here tortures four times a day without any food. Only once a week they are given a spoonful of dirty, earthy water. As it is made of natural earth, it slowly changes the criminals so that they slowly learn the concept of trust. In the iron circle we find many of the famous criminals of Chinese history, together with dishonest businessmen. At the present time, a new section is under construction, we learn in the

---

[30] *Hsieh-to,* 6, 7b–8a.

[31] The Mongol text of 1700 has the Iron City as hell seventeen. after the eight hot and the eight cold hells, as the place where the final judge is, as in our text in hell ten. Samuel Beal, *A Catena of Buddhist Scriptures,* p. 57, also describes the Iron City with a boiling river nearby. This concept is, therefore, quite old, but the position of the Iron City seems to have been subject to change.

book, for the "execution of criminals and the correction of falsehood," which will deal especially with counterfeiters and similar cheaters, whose numbers have increased so much recently.

In hell ten there is also the "city of those who died without cause." Here persons who had been killed without reason or who had been poisoned or who had been forced to commit suicide watch their murderers being punished, and receive satisfaction from this. But as they cannot be reborn until their malefactors are through with their punishment, and as they do not really enjoy the picture they have to see, their condition is not enviable. Of course, persons who died as victims of their loyalty to the state, or because of their piety toward their parents, or faithful widows who preferred suicide to remarriage, will not come to this place, nor will any soldiers be brought to the city of the innocent. Incidentally, it is specifically mentioned that emperors who cause the death of innocent subjects will be punished by loss of life or empire. Finally, we can see in this hell the "blood-dirt-river" which is full of poisonous snakes and serves as a preliminary punishment for women who had abortions or committed infanticide and for monks who violated monastic rules. The behavior of monks seems to have deteriorated in recent times, as there is a new sub-hell in hell nine only for monks who violated the rules of chastity, who smoked, gambled, ate meat, or collected wealth.

This gruesome story of the hells presented in the *Tung-ming pao-chi* leaves out all the details which are often superlative in cruel imagination. It is not without weak spots. For instance, we mentioned already that the author could not find a rationale for the duration of life. Moreover, on the one hand, he implicitly stressed the responsibility of every person for his actions, but on the other hand, he wanted us to believe that some sons, for instance, are of bad character only in order to punish their former malefactor. While an action against a father is normally punished in the most severe fashion, such an action may be only a "revenge action" and as such would not bring forth later punishment. In this example the son is not responsible for his bad behavior because conditions in his former life forced him to act badly in this life.

In all of this several features are especially worthy of note. First, animals are essentially human beings who in this form are receiving punishment for former sins. We read that slaughtered or tortured animals often appear in the hells and try to complain against such unjust treatment—an attempt that is rarely successful.[32] Because animals have human souls it is strictly prohibited by Buddhist law to kill them, because it would be basically the same as killing a human being. But the

[32] *Tung-ming pao-chi,* chap. 21.

mistreatment of an animal apparently does not constitute an evil act, because the animal is a human being, punished for bad acts, and suffering in animal form is its fate. Thus, cruel treatment of animals has been quite common in China, and our books do not contain special laws against it.

A second important concept is that some persons after death become saints in heaven or on earth, that is, super-humans or deities. Such deities or saints are not necessarily Buddhist personalities. They may be Taoist as well. Christianity, as a foreign import, is treated with utmost hostility. There could not be a Christian saint in this system.

A third interesting feature is that there are different categories of ghosts and goblins. Some are souls of persons who committed suicide, as was mentioned above. Some others were criminals who suffered change into ghosts as punishment. Clearly, some of these beings may very well be malevolent and may cause harm to human beings. As a typical example of such a case, the following story might be mentioned:

Mr. Liu, a poor scholar, lives in the temple of Kuan-ti, the god of war. A chicken, belonging to the family of a student, disappears and Mr. Liu is under suspicion of having stolen the chicken and eaten it. To free himself of this suspicion he takes an oath publicly in the temple, saying that his feet should be turned if he has said a lie. He slips, when leaving the temple, and is now so disgraced that he has to leave the city. After further study in Peking, he passes all examinations and reaches a high office. Now he complains against the god for having him unjustly disgraced. An investigation is made and it is found out that on the day of the oath, Kuan-ti had to leave the temple on business. A badger had assumed his role and had tried to make fun of Mr. Liu. The badger is executed by the judge of the netherworld, but Liu erects him a monument; only because he had to leave his home town, he gave up teaching and studied so that he reached high rank.[33]

In this story, the badger either should not have interfered at all or should have saved the innocent scholar from disgrace.

Fourth, while animals are almost like humans, plants are not part of the living world.

Fifth, China is the best place to live; to be reborn in a country other than China is a severe punishment, which can be doubled if one is reborn in animal shape in a foreign country.

Sixth, in some simple way the belief in reincarnation can explain phenomena of population change. There seems to be a concept of a great, but limited, number of souls which at any one moment in history can be found in human or in animal shape, in China or in other countries. Increases in population would indicate an increase in good persons in the

---

[33] *Hsieh-to*, 6, 4b–5a; a similar story, but with a different twist, is in John K. Shyrok, *The Temples of Anking* (Paris, 1931), p. 113.

last generation; decrease, an increase in the number of sinners. A decrease of population may be concomitant with an increase of population in countries outside of China or an increase in the number of animals. But there is also the possibility that it often takes a very long time until a soul is reincarnated. This idea is demonstrated well in a late eighteenth century story:

> Mr. Wang climbed a high mountain and during a thunderstorm entered a cave in which he found a monk in meditation. Out of the head of the monk come, successively and one on top of the other, a military commander, a dog, a civil official, a whore, a child, and a replica of the monk. After these emanations have disappeared at the end of the meditation, the monk explains that this was the series of his last incarnations. He was a general around 400 B.C., was punished for more than a thousand years, until he was reborn as a dog in the tenth century A.D. because of the severity of his sins as general. The next incarnation after life as a dog was in the thirteenth century. Again, for bad conduct the soul had to suffer until the sixteenth century, when it was reborn as a whore as a final part of its punishment. As the whore became pious in later life, she was reborn in the present generation as a child who, after a short life, will be reborn as a monk. The monk seen by Mr. Wang was only a phantom which later could not be found again.[34]

A final observation is the amazingly elaborate institution of the hells whose structure is purely bureaucratic. A great number of offices with a very great number of officials operate according to rules of procedure and according to law. There are promotions and demotions of officials. One amusing story [35] even tells us that recently (pay attention to this indication of change) civil service examinations in the netherworld take place at the same time that they do on earth. Candidates who pass will be promoted, while those who fail will be punished on the "Mountain of Knives" (hell nine in the modern texts). And in the same eighteenth century book we learn that the lists of officials on the staff of various hells are checked from time to time and that at a particular time most of the low employees had escaped to the earth, where they caused harm to human beings working as doctors, whores, or as government officials.[36]

The only difference, compared to the legal procedure on earth, is that the social status of the accused or the plaintiff is not taken into consideration and justice operates according to objective standards, applied by correct, incorrupt, and usually reliable officials. There was, we learn, a total of 149 hells and sub-hells in hells one to nine, to which three special divisions of hell ten (see above) have to be added, that is, 152 hells, each with an office, a director, and a staff. The highest ruler over this

---

[34] *Hsieh-to,* 9, 5a–6a.
[35] *Ibid.,* 2, 6b–7b.
[36] *Ibid.,* 6, 1b–2a.

vast personnel is the Jade Emperor (Yü Huang-ti), who corresponds to the emperor in this world and who can commute individual sentences.

Just as on earth not all criminals are immediately caught and punished, so it can happen in the netherworld, especially if the criminals are ghosts. The following story from the beginning of the nineteenth century is interesting in this respect, but also provides insight into sexual habits and beliefs.

Mr. Ch'in Hsiu's father, an official, died, but as he had been honest, he left no money, so that the son could not bury him and stored the coffin in a temple while he went to his maternal uncle Chang. Ch'in Hsiu, at that time around eighteen years of age, had a friend, Yin, whose wife had died. Yin had tried for three years to see her in his dreams, but in vain. The Changs had a seventeen-year-old daughter who also died. Ch'in befriended himself with an age-mate, young Mr. Huang, and against the warning of Huang's parents, both young men visited a house of prostitution. Each of them selected a very beautiful girl and they went to separate chambers. Not much later, Huang raised loud complaints. Ch'in rose and noticed that, instead of the beauty, he had an ugly girl in his bed. The girl immediately asked him not to raise complaints and to stop his friend. The house was locked, she said, and there were some seven pimps in the house who always changed the girls. Whoever complained was murdered by them. Ch'in and his friend kept quiet and they learned that the pimps would be out during the next night, in which they could get the girls they wanted. In the morning they did not complain and offered the money to the pimps, who were kind and refused to accept any money. The next night they returned and each got a beautiful girl. Before going to bed, Ch'in's girl said she wanted to introduce herself and said her name was Yin. Ch'in now realized that she was the dead wife of his best friend. Huang, to whom the same happened, found himself with his cousin, the dead Miss Chang. Ch'in was startled and asked what was going on. Mrs. Yin explained that the pimps were ghosts too. Ghosts, belonging to the other world, consist of only the element Yin (the female element) and cannot have normal sexual relations. So they set up the establishment, and with the help of the beautiful girls they induced young men to come, and then exchanged the girls. After intercourse, they took the semen from the ugly girls and ate it. As semen is pure Yang element, they got strength and their penises became bigger than normal. Now they violated the beautiful girls, causing them much pain. Ch'in, outraged, asked what he could do against this unlawful behavior. Mrs. Yin said he should go to the city-god of Su-chou and complain. Ch'in, whose home was not in Su-chou, raised objections toward bothering a foreign city-god, but Mrs. Yin declared that the god was his own father, appointed to this high office because of his honesty.

Both boys told the story to the parents Chang and to Mr. Yin. Mr. Yin now understood why he could not see his wife in his dreams, and the Changs cried bitterly. All of them went to the city and slept in the temple. They heard the rattle of instruments of torture, and heard the girls testifying one after the other. Each girl gave the name of the ghost who had violated her. The unfortunate Miss Chang had been violated by all of the ghosts. The god, old Mr. Ch'in, serving as judge, asked Miss Chang to go to the private

apartments in the temple to meet Mrs. Ch'in, her aunt and young Ch'in's
mother. Then the ghosts were punished, especially as Miss Chang had asked
the death penalty for all of them. Our sleepers, now convinced of the terrible
fate which had come over their relatives, wept bitterly. In the next night,
Mrs. Yin visited her husband in a dream and stated that she felt too much
ashamed of the adultery to which she had been forced, to communicate
further with him, and said good-bye to Yin. Miss Chang saw Huang—with
whom she had had intercourse while Ch'in had had intercourse with the wife
of his friend—quite often in his dreams. The house of prostitution was, of
course, a cemetery, as the friends had found out on the morning after.[37]

The important element in this story is the interweaving of both worlds
and the continuation of family relations in both worlds: the judge is the
hero's father, yet he judges objectively. Family relationship only makes
contacts easier.

Pictures of the Hells

It was already remarked that some books, like the *Yü-li*, are illustrated. The illustrations, more or less simple woodcuts, depict the main
punishments in the different hells. These illustrations seem to have a long
history and deserve a special study. I shall here only call attention to
certain points.

According to tradition, the earliest pictures of hells in China proper,
and at the same time the most famous ones, were made in 736[38] by the
renowned painter Wu Tao-tse in the Ching-kung temple in Ch'ang-an,
the capital of China at the time. Later texts assert that hell paintings by
Wu Tao-tse were in a temple on the P'an-lung mountain in Feng-tu district in Szu-ch'uan, the "Polar Hell" (*Pei-chi ti-yü*) of the Taoists.[39]
T'ang and Sung texts often refer to paintings of the punishments in hell,[40]
but one does not know what they looked like. Wu Tao-tse's paintings are
not preserved. We assume that they were murals, painted on temple
walls.

The earliest existing Chinese paintings are on scrolls of the thirteenth
century.[41] They seem to have portrayed one hell on each painting;

[37] *Erh-shih lu,* 2, 9a–10b.

[38] See Edouard Chavannes, *Le T'ai chan,* (Paris, 1910), p. 356, note; also *T'ang
hua-tuan,* as quoted in *T'ai-p'ing kuang-chi,* 212, Vol. 17, p. 5a.

[39] *I-chien-chih,* 48, 1b.

[40] *Kuang-i-chi,* quoted in *T'ai-p'ing kuang-chi,* 444, Vol. 36, p. 19a, and *I-
chien-chih,* 31, 8a.

[41] See Kojiro Tomita, *Portfolio of Chinese Paintings* (Boston, 1933), Plates
106–109, and *Bijutsu Kenkyu,* Vol. 45 (1935), plates on pp. 425 and 424, and
Plate XI. I am grateful to Professor Aschwin Lippe, who called my attention to
these publications.

perhaps some other paintings of deities serving in hells originally belonged to the same set.[42] These scrolls are of good quality and serious intent. They depict the judges as stern officials; and the procedures in hell, although gruesome, are painted with more restraint than in later, popular paintings. To judge from the modern usage of similar scrolls, these paintings may have been used only during funeral ceremonies and funeral masses in private homes; they were usually in storage and not exhibited even in temples. As far as details are recognizable in these paintings, they agree better with the standard modern texts than do the modern paintings, where certain scenes, known from the texts and from the old scrolls, are not represented. I have seen scrolls of only one set of modern, popular paintings of the punishments in hell, for use in funeral ceremonies [43] in Taiwan. The set consists of five paintings. Hells one and ten are on individual scrolls; all other scrolls depict two hells each. This set deviates greatly from all other sets of hell pictures known to me; I presume that either the painter was quite unfamiliar with the texts or he had an incomplete set of pictures as a model. Thus, he mixed up the hells, depicting punishments in hells where, according to the texts, they did not belong.

Hell pictures are painted, of course, not only on scrolls but also on walls of many temples in traditional as well as modern non-Communist China. In modern Taiwan, sets of hell pictures appear most often in the temple of the city god (Ch'eng-huang),[44] the God of the Eastern Peak (Tung-yüeh), or the temple for Ti-tsang—temples of deities who are involved in the punishment of sinners. In some temples, the paintings are not frescoes, but pictures hung on the walls. We find these pictures in different arrangements. A set of six panels from a temple in Tainan [45] has hells two, three, and five, and seven, nine, and ten, together on one panel, while the other hells have individual panels. The paintings in the Ti-tsang-en in Hsin-chuang near Taipei consist of four panels: hells one and two, three to five, six to eight, and nine and ten are put together.

[42] Plate XI is a picture of the Niu-t'ou (Ox-head), an accompanying figure, serving in hell.

[43] I am grateful to Professor Arthur P. Wolf, who made the photographs available to me. The scrolls were used in Taipei, but it is unknown where and when they were painted. I heard that such paintings are still produced in Taiwan for use in funerals, but I was unable to buy any in spite of several attempts.

[44] I saw a set in the city god temple of Chin-yün (Chekiang) on October 2, 1934. Similar frescoes are mentioned in *Monumenta Serica*, Vol. 13, p. 236. The *T'ai-shang pao-fa t'u shuo*, 8, p. 34a, mentions a set of eighteen paintings in a temple of the T'ai-shan god. There were explanatory texts to the frescoes. Brunhild Körner possessed once a full set of which only one painting is preserved. B. Körner, *Die religiöse Welt der Bäuerin in Nord-China* (Stockholm, 1959).

[45] I am obliged to Dr. Martin Gimm, who sent me the set from the Tung-yüeh-tien in Tainan City.

The First Hell. (Print from Shanghai, undated, probably around 1920)

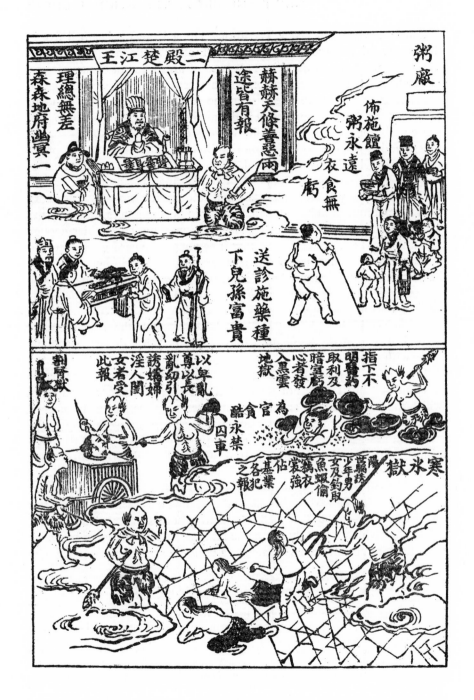

The Second Hell. (Print from Shanghai, undated, probably around 1920)

A temple in Sha-t'ien (New Territories, Hong Kong) [46] has hell five in the center of a large painting, and all other hells are arranged in semicircular fashion around it. This kind of arrangement occurs also on loose sheets that are for sale, on which often the wheel of incarnation (belonging to hell number ten) is in the center.[47] The decision in favor of this or any other arrangement is definitely related to considerations of space and money: in some temples there is only a limited space—or the space made available to the painter is limited. As for money, the prices of commercial paintings are calculated according to size and number of individual panels; since donors of temple paintings usually give a specific amount of money, which may be small, the painter may have to work with a minimum number of panels. In addition, painters take liberties with regard to the texts, either because they may not be familiar enough with the tradition, or because neither they nor the general public seem to be particularly concerned about accuracy. In practice, then, the artist has considerable freedom. As a result, of course, for those familiar with the texts the temple paintings are full of "mistakes," often depicting punishments in hells in which they do not belong; the modern pictures of punishments in hell do not necessarily agree with the corresponding texts. But then, even the pictures illustrating the Yü-li do not absolutely agree with the text!

In addition to paintings and frescoes, hell scenes occur also as reliefs in temples,[48] but I have not seen a full set, only a set of two panels in which the punishment of sinners is contrasted with the treatment of good people. Presumably hell scenes also have been depicted with fully sculptured statues—in one case described as provided with a hidden mechanism to put them into motion, a trick which naturally frightened many temple visitors.[49]

Besides all these paintings on scrolls and temple walls, there are the illustrations in the texts mentioned above. In most of these books two pictures are devoted to each hell: one picture shows the punishments, the other one (which is usually above the first one) shows activities by which a sinner can redeem his sins. Usually, a book illustration is provided with

[46] I am obliged to Professor Jack Potter, who photographed the painting in the Kuan-yin temple in Sha-t'ien, after I had copied the inscriptions.

[47] Howard R. Long, *The People of Mushan* (Columbia, Miss., 1960). Woo Chan Cheng, *Érotologie de la Chine* (Paris, 1963), p. 146, reproduces one picture of a set of two, printed in the late nineteenth century and depicting hells one to five.

[48] For instance, on the wall of the outside of the Sen-lo Hall on top of the Shih-t'ou-shan near Hsin-chu, Taiwan, seen March 15, 1964.

[49] *Su-t'an*, reprinted in *Li-tai hsiao-shuo pi-chi hsüan;* Ming texts, Vol. 1, p. 34. Temples like the Tung-yüeh Miao in Peking sometimes have sculptures of the judges and jailers, but not of the punished sinners.

a legend indicating clearly the kind of sin and punishment depicted. Some of the frescoes also have brief texts. None of the funeral scrolls seems to be provided with a text, but in order to identify the hell, the name of the hell and of its judge is written on a board painted as though hanging above the entrance to the hall in which the judge sits and in front of which all activities go on. The Sung scrolls do not yet have halls with inscriptions above the entrances.

As already mentioned, the texts differ from one another, and so do the illustrations. From a comparison of all pictures known to me,[50] it appears that in most cases three characteristic punishments are shown for each hell, and more details are given only if space allows. The picture of the first hell shows normally the terrace from which one can see one's sins, and the mirror in which the sins are reflected; [51] an assistant to the judge with a book of accounts; one warden, who is either the Niu-t'ou (Ox-head) with an ox-head, or a wild-looking strong man with weapons. Occasionally, starving people and a dark house for the repair of torn books are shown.[52]

The pictures of the second hell typically show punishment in a frozen lake; [53] a man in a narrow cage with only his head sticking out; and a man who is castrated or whose tongue is cut off. Occasionally a punishment in a dark place is shown.

Characteristic for hell number three is the cutting out of the heart or the intestines; people tied to red-hot copper pipes; and a butcher butchering human beings. Occasionally, tigers and ghosts are shown devouring people.

In hell number four one usually sees people turned into powder, either by a mortar like a South Chinese rice mortar, or by a mill resembling the North Chinese wheat mills. Dogs then devour the powder. The "city of those who died without deserving it" (Wang szu ch'eng) occurs here, although the texts put it into another hell; furthermore, people are conducted to a place of execution. Occasionally a kind of gallows is shown on which two persons are hanging.

[50] This includes two editions of the Yü-li, the old edition of the Yü-li by G. W. Clarke, and the pictures given by Henry Doré.

[51] The reliefs mentioned in note 48 above show in one scene the mirror and in another one the treatment of the good.

[52] A set of ten large paintings in the Sen-lo Hall on top of the Shih-t'ou-shan near Hsin-chu, Taiwan, has Niu-t'ou and Ma-mien (Horse-face) twice; for the first time they occur in hell three; the second time they are in their traditional place in hell five. This set puts the mending of books into hell eight, in which it does not belong, according to the texts. The ten paintings mentioned here are quite new, but undated. They start with hell number one in the rear on the right side wall and number six on the left side wall, so that visitors first see hells number five and number ten, and two most spectacular and important hells.

[53] The Sen-lo Hall paintings (see n. 52) put the ice lake in hell three.

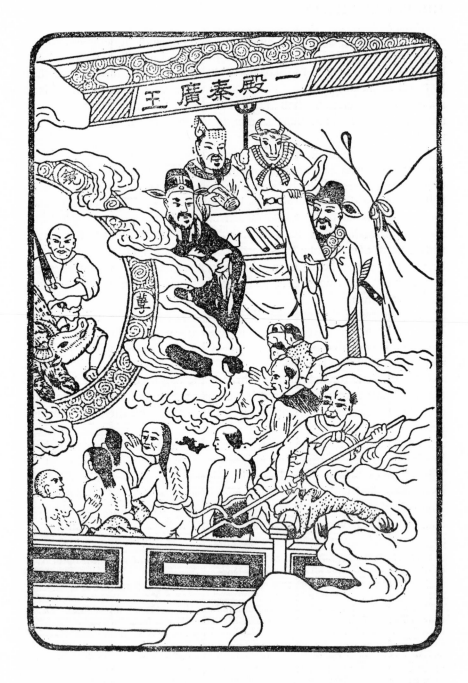

The First Hell. (*From a copy of the* Yü-li pao-ch'ao, *printed in Taichung 1963*)

The Second Hell. Compare the armed gaolers and the person in the cangue with those shown in the frontispiece. (From a copy of the Yü-li pao-ch'ao, *printed in Taichung 1963)*

Typical for hell number five are the picture of a man cut into two pieces by a kind of guillotine; the building called the "terrace for looking back home" (*Wang-hsiang t'ai*), and two prison officials, normally Niu-t'ou (*Ox-head*) and Ma-mien (*Horse-face*), but sometimes the two ghosts who snatch the souls. In addition, some pictures show people changed into animal shape or people wearing the cangue,[54] a yokelike structure used to punish criminals.

Hell number six has the upright-board saw in which persons are split lengthwise from head to foot; people tied to a scaffold like a cross and in the process of being cut up; a bed of nails. Sometimes a scene is added in which people kneel on iron scrapings.

The seventh hell has the oil kettle, the fire lake, and the cutting of the tongue.[55]

The eighth hell has a scene in which a man is crushed by a cart, and a large picture of the "lake of blood and pus" with its bridge.[56]

The ninth hell shows a kettle in which persons are boiled, people being eaten by birds, and the knife mountain. In the series of Sung paintings the ninth hell shows how people are fed to goats; this scene has disappeared from most modern paintings,[57] but is mentioned in modern texts.

The tenth and final hell shows the judge with two officials of whom one usually carries a book and the other an abacus. In front of them are people who are changing into animals; and to the side is the *nai-ho* bridge across a river full of snakes and vermin. If the animals are not shown, the large "wheel of incarnations" is painted, from which different categories of beings emanate in different directions.

In summary, there are two traditions of hell painting. The first is represented by the paintings on scrolls, for use in temples or in funeral processions, and by the frescoes and other pictures in temples. The

---

[54] A single scene, depicting Yen-lo-wang, the head of this hell, with Niu-t'ou and Ma-mien, occurs in several Taiwanese temples. This scene always has a Huo-wu-ch'ang, a policeman of hell, who catches the sinners and brings them to the judge; often he is accompanied by Chung K'ui, who has a similar function. In the scene there is also an official, the sinner, in a cangue, an instrument of torture consisting of a large board fastened around the neck. This scene was found in the Ti-tsang-en in Hsin-chuang, Taiwan (March 28, 1964), above the entrance to the side shrine on the right side. It was also found in the Chung-shun miao in Mu-shan near Taipei (April 1, 1964) and in the Pao-an kung in Taipei (March 19, 1964). The scene is most likely a scene from a theater play, but I have been unable to identify the play. The best-known play in which punishments in hell are shown is a shadow-play built on the basis of the Mu-lien story (not in Grube's texts; I saw the play on April 24, 1935, in Peking).

[55] The Sen-lo Hall paintings have this scene in hell number five.

[56] This lake is in hell number six in the Sen-lo Hall set.

[57] It is found in the Sen-lo Hall paintings in hell number ten.

Probable representation of the First Hell. Relief from the walls of a temple in Hsin-chu, Taiwan. (Photograph by the author 1964)

The Second, Third, and Fifth Hells. The person in the cangue corresponds to the similar figure shown in the frontispiece. From a wall painting in a temple in Taiwan. (Photograph by Professor M. Gimm 1960)

First Hell. From a scroll in San Francisco. Date unknown. (Photograph by E. Moody)

second tradition is represented by the illustrations in books dealing with sins, usually woodcuts or lithographs. The traditions are not identical, although they surely influenced each other.[58] The temple artist is largely free, but considerations of space and money are important. No one expects that temple visitors or participants in a funeral procession will look to see whether the pictures completely agree with what they may have read in books. Every individual scene is lively and cruel enough to serve as a warning. It is too early to say whether changes have occurred over time in the content of the paintings; there were stylistic changes, of course. At first sight is seems that the older paintings are more sedate and the newer paintings more sadistic, but this impression may be due to an unfair comparison—a comparison between an old painting made by a respectable painter, and a modern one made by a commercial artist.

Temples Concerned with Hells

TEMPLES FOR THE GOD OF THE EAST MOUNTAIN

Edouard Chavannes has shown in a long and beautiful study [59] that ancient China had a cult of sacred mountains and that the cult of the Tung-yüeh (East Mountain), which is the T'ai-shan in Shantung province, was one of the liveliest centers of this cult. He has also shown that in later periods the mountain became connected with the concepts of death and punishment. The god of the Tung-yüeh became a judge of the dead. In time, this concept spread all over China, and Tung-yüeh temples were built in almost all big centers. At the same time this god came to be regarded as king or judge of the seventh hell, where he meted out rather harsh punishments—a more specialized function, in which he was called T'ai-shan wang (king of the T'ai-shan). When these developments took place is hard to decide, but Tung-yüeh temples certainly were built before 900. My temple survey for Central and South China,[60] which deals with almost 12,000 temples, has 76 references to Tung-yüeh temples; this number includes all such temples, old and new, rebuilt or repaired, or renamed. The references indicate that there were three periods of great building activity in the field of Tung-yüeh temples: (a)

[58] I know from interviews with Taiwanese temple painters that commercial temple painters use books as source of inspiration if they did not learn from their teachers how to paint certain scenes or if they do not remember theater scenes well enough to reproduce them. (Interviews conducted in Taipei and in Tainan, 1964.)

[59] Edouard Chavannes, Le T'ai chan (Paris, 1910).

[60] To be published in Monumenta Serica, 1966.

1250–1300, (b) 1600–1800, (c) 1850–1900. This pattern deviates to some degree from the general pattern of temple building. The first period of interest in Tung-yüeh temples was about fifty years earlier than a general peak in temple building. The second period began slightly later than a general rise in renewed interest. And the last period was much more pronounced for Tung-yüeh temples than for other temples. Interestingly enough, it is after 1850 that many more books and larger editions of books dealing with sin and punishment began to be published. This means that in a period of definite crisis, characterized by the T'ai-p'ing rebellion and the conflicts with Western powers, and expressed by the destruction of innumerable other temples, special attention was given to Tung-yüeh temples. The situation was similar in the two previous periods of high interest in Tung-yüeh temples. The years after 1250 can also be conceived as years of crisis: the final defeat of the Sung dynasty and the establishment of the foreign rule of Mongols over China. And in 1644, again a Chinese dynasty was dethroned, and the foreign rule of the Manchu was instituted.

Tung-yüeh temples are distinguished by different names. It seems that at first there was the Tung-yüeh miao (Temple of the [God of the] East Mountain) on the T'ai-shan. Elsewhere the earliest name was *Tung-yüeh hsing-kung*, Travel Palace of the (God of the) East Mountain. Materials other than our temple survey show that around the year 1200 a great number of *hsing-kung* were constructed in the urban centers of Middle China.[61] It is quite evident that the god was believed to have his permanent residence on the T'ai-shan in the Tung-yüeh miao but that when traveling through the country, he would live in his "travel palaces." This designation remained quite common in South China, while Central China soon began to prefer the designation *Tung-yüeh miao*. In my survey I was able to date *"miao"* from the beginning of the twelfth century in Central China. The idea that the god could have a permanent seat in any city was developed in that area apparently quite early. *Miao* also indicates that the god was to some degree regarded as similar to other popular, so-called Taoist deities. On the other hand, the designation *kuan,* indicating a strictly Taoist temple or monastery, has been rarely used for this god.

[61] A temple was enlarged around 1150 in Tsih-chou, Szu-ch'uan (*I-wen tsung-lu*, 2, 2b–3a); around 1200 there was one in Ch'ang-chou, Kiangsu (*I-chien-chih*, 22, 4a), in Jao-chou, Kiangsi (*ibid.*, 9, 3a), and in nearby Po-yang, Kiangsi (*ibid.*, 36, 5a); around 1150 in Hsia-chou, Hupei (*ibid.*, 11, 3a); in 1172 a temple was built in Lien-shui, Kiangsu (*ibid.*, 27, 3b); we hear of one in Hu-k'ou near Ching-tê-chen in Kiangsi in 1190 (*ibid.*, 40, 8b). There were five temples in Hangchow in Sung time (*Meng-liang lu*, 14, 5a), one in Yen-p'ing, Fukien (*I-chien-chih*, 38, 8b) and one in Hua-t'ing, Kiangsu (*ibid.*, 39, 6b).

The builders of Tung-yüeh temples were private persons or government officials, with the difference that in Central China more temples
were built by private persons while in South China more were built by
government officials. This apparent difference may result, however, from
a difference in time, since many Southern temples were built later than
the temples in Central China.

The Tung-yüeh temples have always been places of intimidation and
horror. Typically, the walls are painted with those pictures of the punishments in hell which were described above. One temple in Ch'ang-shu
(Kiangsu) [62] in Ming time had no pictures, but there were large-scale
statues which could be moved by a hidden system of levers and which
then enacted gruesome activities. The mechanism operated automatically
as soon as a person entered the temple and stepped on the levers. People
did not dare to enter this temple during darkness.

These temples can be inside as well as outside the cities; while the
"travel palaces" seem to have been more often on mountains outside,
many were also inside towns; many a town had more than one *Tung-
yüeh miao*. Hangchou had already in Sung time five such temples.

Since Sung time it was believed that the god had his birthday on the
twenty-eighth day of the third month. On this day, religious organizations created for the purpose set up a big temple mass.[63] Down to the
early twentieth century, there was a special mass in the Tung-yüeh
temple in Peking on this day.[64] There is only one text known to me in
which the twenty-seventh, and not the twenty-eighth, day is the god's
birthday.[65] The celebrations were connected with healing: in Peking
people touched the figure of a donkey made of bronze in order to get
rid of eye, ear, and other diseases.[66] Already around 1200 the Tung-yüeh
temple in Ch'ang-chou (Kiangsu) was connected with disease, in this
case with small pox.[67] The logical connection here is probably that the
god could send disease to sinners and that persons with a disease might
get healed if they prayed for forgiveness to the god.

TEMPLES FOR TI-TSANG AND MU-LIEN

The next two deities most closely connected with the idea of sin and
punishment are Ti-tsang (Ksittigarbha) and Mu-lien. In the tradition of
Anhui, Ti-tsang is regarded as the ruler over all hells, the boss of the

[62] *Su-t'an;* see *Li-tai hsiao-shuo pi-chi hsüan; Ming,* Vol. 1, pp. 33–34.
[63] *Meng-liang lu,* 2, 4a; *Wu-lin chiu-shih,* 3, 2b.
[64] Grube, *Pekinger Volkskunde,* p. 64.
[65] *Yü-li (chih) pao ch'ao,* p. 53.
[66] *Pei-p'ing huai-ku,* p. 20.
[67] *I-chien-chih,* 22, 4a.

judges of hell. When, according to the novel *Hsi-yo-chi,* the divine monkey threatened the divine kings, they complained to Ti-tsang.[68] Ti-tsang has always been connected in Chinese folk belief with Korea.[69] Since T'ang times, his most famous temple was on top of the Chiu-hua Mountain in Ch'ing-yang, close to the present city of Wu-hu in Anhui. Here, it is reported,[70] Korean monks lived and practiced geophagy. This temple is mentioned in a Ming drama,[71] and another Ming drama [72] mentions Ti-tsang in connection with a story much like the Mu-lien story, further below.

My temple survey has twenty-three references to temples especially built for Ti-tsang. The first references are for South China: in the year 911 a temple was built in Chien-ning (Fukien), and in 1132 another one was built in Hai-yang (Kuangtung). But Ti-tsang temples seem to be equally common all over China. In seventeen cases, his temples were called *en*—they were small and might be connected with nunneries. Only the earlier Ti-tsang temples had other names such as *yüan* or *sih*. No Ti-tsang temple in our survey was built by an official; six were built by citizens and three by monks. This indicates that Ti-tsang's cult was mainly a popular cult and not specifically sponsored by government officials. Temples for Ti-tsang were quite common in the Chinese–Mongolian borderland of Chahar from the fourteenth century.[73]

Ti-tsang temples can be built in connection with other temples. There was, for instance, in the Kuan-yin temple complex in Yang-chou a temple for Ti-tsang and next to it a hall for the ten judges of hell.[74]

Mu-lien was a pious Buddhist who attempted to save his mother from the punishments in hell, as we heard above (p. 25), and who, according to some traditions, eventually became Ti-tsang.[75] He, too, had several temples. In our survey, the oldest one was in Hsia-p'u (Fukien), renamed with his name in 954, rebuilt in 972, and for the last time, in 1915. There was still another temple for him in Hsia-p'u, but undated. Otherwise, we have only a 1608 temple for him in P'u-t'ien (Fukien) and an undated temple in Hsiang-shan (Kuangtung). My survey contains no special temple for him in Central China. In general, Mu-lien seems not to have been so important that many temples were built for him alone.

---

[68] Both pieces of information according to H. Doré, *Recherches sur les Superstitions en Chine,* Vol. 6, p. 157.

[69] *Ibid.*

[70] Early texts quoted in *Ch'ü-hai,* I, 444–447 in notes.

[71] *Ho-sha chi* (see *Ch'ü-hai,* I, 444–447).

[72] *Hua-lung hui* (see *Ch'ü-hai,* I, 481–485).

[73] W. Grootaers in *Monumenta Serica,* 13, pp. 277–281.

[74] *Yang-chou hua-fang lu,* chap. 16, p. 366 (eighteenth century).

[75] Grube, *Pekinger Volkskunde,* p. 56.

This brief note on temples connected with sin may serve to show that a further study of temples, even if only of names of temples, is needed. It may give better insight into the spread of certain attitudes and beliefs,[76] including the belief in the punishment of sins.

Conclusion

A recent survey which I made in Taiwan [77] shows that none of the religious books that describe sins and their punishment is among the popular religious texts. Yet we have reasons to assume that most common people in China had some knowledge of the content of these books. They could get this knowledge, in addition, from such popular ballads as we found in Taiwan in printed versions.[78] They could further hear about the punishments by seeing one of the numerous plays which show the deeds of Mu-lien.[79] Such plays were also produced as shadow plays, and most likely as movies, too.[80] Finally, the visitor of temples could see the pictures of the punishments as scrolls on the temple walls, as frescoes or reliefs on beams and panels of temples. And he would remember them, if he visited temples specifically devoted to deities in relation to the hells. Thus, there can be no doubt that every common man and woman in some way was exposed to these doctrines and was, perhaps, influenced by them.

[76] My survey of temples contains, for instance, a certain number of temples whose names contain references to ritual cleanliness, a concept whose importance is shown in chapter iii. A great number of other temples contain references to peace: it seems clear that such a name for a temple was given preference at the beginning of a new dynasty, i.e., after a long period of wars, in the hope that peace would soon prevail.

[77] "Religious Activities and Religious Books in Modern China," in *Zeitschrift für Missionswissenschaft* (1965), No. 4, pp. 260–269.

[78] See note 16 above.

[79] Most popular is *Mu-lien chiu-mu,* but there are many other plays, such as *Hua-yo shan, Lo-pu miao-jung, Hsiang-mei sih, Mu-lien,* etc., which describe parts of this story.

[80] I saw a Japanese movie with the title *Ti-yü* (Hell) in Kyoto, August 17, 1960.

CHAPTER THREE

The Categories of Sin and Changes in the Concept of Sin

There is no doubt that the basic content of even so recent a book as the *Tung-ming pao-chi* is derived from a Buddhist source quite similar to the *Cheng-fa nien-ch'u ching* which, again, is derived from an original Indian source.

Although we have much historical material for Chinese cultural history, it has always been difficult to prove changes that are more than philological emendations on the basis of standard ceremonial texts. It might be easier to prove change by studying how people behaved in life situations. In our case, it is enticing to study the change of the concept of sin over one-and-a-half millennia, but such an enterprise meets with a number of problems. One of these is that most intermediate texts representing the same line of tradition are incomplete. Secondly, the different texts deviate so strongly from one another that a line-by-line comparison is not possible. The names of the different hells remain the same (and these names go back to original Indian names), but the structure of the hells varies. Table 1 presents an abstract of the character of the hells in two older Buddhist sources and in two modern sources. We have mentioned already that the modern sources have added one initial sorting-and-arranging hell, and one final hell, so that the numbers are not the same, while the names are identical.

For classificatory purposes, we can divide the sins into four groups. The first group consists of sexual sins. These include also transgressions which have to do with ritual impurity. We came to the belief that pollution is the main concept behind many, if not most, sexual sins. The second group comprises sins against the person—social sins. Technically, sexual sins often tend to fall into this category. But because of the importance of the problem of sex we decided to separate sexual sins from sins in which the body of another person is damaged or destroyed. The third group includes sins against property, and in the fourth group there are sins against deities or supernatural beings.

On the other hand, it is possible to set up a kind of grading system. As punishment in each hell is more severe than in the preceding hell, one can set up a point-scale of transgressions. The higher the "point average" the more severe the punishment. This attempt has two weaknesses. Some sins are punished in more than one hell. There are even crimes so severe that the sinner receives punishment in each of the hells for his sin, and rebirth afterward in human shape is impossible for seemingly endless periods. We have in all such cases taken into calculation only the last hell in which punishment is mentioned, not all earlier hells. Secondly, since the numbering is not identical in the old and the new texts, we have, for the sake of uniformity, diminished the number of the hells in the new texts by one. The results of our procedure are presented in Tables 1, 2, and 3.

Three somewhat composite points are immediately clear. First, the older texts stress sins against deities or their property much more than the recent texts, and are preoccupied with Buddhist religious concepts, while the recent texts emphasize the basic Confucian ethical precepts dealing mainly with interpersonal relations. Thus, the percentage of social sins is much higher in the modern texts than in the old texts. The grade-point average of social sins is also much higher in the modern texts. Secondly, sexual sins are more prominent in the early texts, but their grade-point average is lower than in the modern texts, mainly because many of the sexual sins in the old texts are relatively light sins. Thirdly, among the social sins the crimes against the state or the government play almost no role in the old text, but some role in the modern texts.

Let us now look more closely into the different kinds of sins in the old and the new texts.

Sexual Sins

The *Cheng-fa,* the oldest of our books, has one set of sexual sins consisting of unnatural ways of intercourse (grade point: 3) or of intercourse with animals (3). Adultery is severely punished if the adulterer talks about it so that the woman is punished (5). All other sexual sins are directly in relation to religion: monks who think of sex instead of religion are relatively lightly punished (3), but seduction or rape of women by monks, or of nuns by men who turn the interest of women

TABLE 1

GENERAL CHARACTER OF PUNISHMENTS

Text: *Cheng-fa, circa* A.D. 500	*Catena*		*Tung-ming* (20th cent.)	*Yü-li* (19th cent.)
Hell 1: Killing	General sins	2:	Sex; cheating; bad family relations; bad doctors	Sex; cheating; bad doctors
Hell 2: Stealing	Against priests; against religion	3:	Against 5 Confucian principles; stealing	Against state, government; stealing
Hell 3: Sexual sins	Wicked persons	4:	Asocial; theft; cheating	Asocial, non-payment of taxes
Hell 4: Drinking	Murder	5:	Against Buddhist religion; sex; arson; against family	Against Buddhist religion; arson
Hell 5: Calumnies	Heresy	6:	Against gods, Buddhism, parents, political	Against government
Hell 6: False religion (sexual aspect)	Killing animals	7:	Love potions; calumnies	Love potions
Hell 7: Against Buddhism	"Turning to evil"	8:	Against 5 family rules of Confucianism, sex; banditry	Against 5 Confucian rules
Hell 8: Against Buddhism	Worst sins	9:	Sex magic; 5 worst sins of state	Five worst sins; sex magic

TABLE 2

DISTRIBUTION OF SINS
(in percentages)

Type:	Cheng-fa	Yü-li	Tung-ming
	(n = 111)	(n = 142)	(n = 313)
Sexual	32.4	19.0	19.5
Social	10.8	32.4	34.8
Property	21.6	33.8	30.0
Deities	35.2	14.8	15.7
	100.0	100.0	100.0

TABLE 3

POINT AVERAGE OF SINS

Type:	Cheng-fa	Yü-li	Tung-ming
	(n = 111)	(n = 142)	(n = 313)
Sexual	5.0[a] (36)[b]	5.5 (27)	5.3 (61)
Social	2.7 (12)	3.6 (46)	5.1 (109)
Property	4.6 (24)	3.5 (48)	4.7 (94)
Deities	6.0 (39)	5.0 (21)	5.3 (49)

[a] Figures in grade points 1-8
[b] Figures in parentheses are number of cases

from religion to sex, are considered much more severe sins (7). The worst sin is a sexual act with a Buddhist saint (8). Homosexuality is regarded as a sin (3), and the use of wine as a way to seduce women is an aggravating factor (4). Incest is a severe sin (7), and if incest is committed with the mother under the influence of wine, the sin is still worse (8). Interestingly, incest with sisters in countries where this is the custom [1] is relatively lightly punished (3) in the *Cheng-fa*. The aspect of ritual uncleanliness is relatively unimportant. For instance, persons who give unclean food, especially to monks, are reborn as "hungry spirits" (*preta*), but no specific punishment in the hells before rebirth is mentioned.

A textual fragment of the *Mu-lien* story, found in Tun-huang and written in 921 A.D., which describes only five hells, already stresses further categories of sexual sins: intercourse on the bed of the parents, the teacher, or the master (grade point: 3), as well as transvestism (3).

---

[1] This seems to refer to endogamous practices in the Himalayan areas.

Here, the essence of the sin is the concept of the ritual impurity of the sex act.

The modern texts, *Yü-li* and *Tung-ming,* are strongly against incest (grade point: 6.3), mention homosexuality briefly (8), but have a large array of sexual sins of a nonreligious kind. They are against abortions and the killing of baby daughters, adultery, rape, and fornication, especially of married women, but typically most of the sexual sins are committed by women, who try to seduce men, have love affairs, are jealous of the husband's concubines, are disobedient so that they spoil the reputation of the family, or do not keep the rules of the harem. Some sinful women even go so far as to try to get a divorce or to behave as if they had equality with men. Sexual-religious sins are much rarer in the modern texts: violation of nuns or monks is mentioned (4.5), as is the performing of religious ceremonies in which either the food taboos are violated or the sacrificer thinks of sex instead of religion. Only once are monks mentioned who have sex affairs with nuns or with ordinary Buddhists (8). Whorehouses and the selling of girls into houses of prostitution, on the other hand, are mentioned several times (7). But while these sins in the area of sex already indicate a strong influence of Chinese customs modifying the Indian tendencies in the old text, the modern texts excel in two categories: there are a great number of sins in the area of uncleanliness and in the area of sex medicines and other stimulants.

Ritual uncleanliness consists of such acts as depositing garbage in front or in the rear of temples, monasteries, and pagodas; sacrificing to the kitchen god when kitchen and hearth are dirty; or sacrificing during the period of menstruation; washing menstrual laundry in running water or pouring such water close to the hearth or the well; drying menstrual laundry in open sunshine. It is equally serious to urinate or defecate toward the north, to have intercourse with direction to the well, the hearth, the north; to have intercourse in temples, monasteries, under the open sky at day time or during moonshine at night, or simply to expose the genitals toward the moon or the stars. Related to such sins are those which consist of giving unclean food to parents, husbands, and deities.

It is clear from these cases that the modern Chinese feel strongly that bodily functions and especially sexual acts are unclean and should be hidden, a trait which began to appear already in the tenth century text. This aspect should be stressed especially because many books on China try to give the impression that sex is something "quite natural" and unproblematic among the Chinese, as long as it is "normal" and occurs among persons who are not forbidden by law or taboo to have sexual relations. The other new category, also very extensive, deals with the preparation of love potions, sex drugs, and implements for unnatural sex acts. Here we find, as a special group, drugs for the prolongation of life or sexual strength, made of sexual organs, fetuses, human flesh or bones. Closely related with such sins are the sins consisting of writing books on sex, and immoral novels, stories, or songs full of sex. Also painting—even making decorations on bed sheets or other textiles with sexual or religious symbols—is sinful. But it is also a sin to apply symbols of religious character to bed sheets or pillows, because they will be defaced and soiled. Open talk about love affairs or peeping into the harems of others is sinful. People should read moralistic books, and persons who do not read such books, and make fun of them, or destroy them, commit serious sins.

Again, the element of "impurity" is strong in all these sins. Confucian books never talk about sexual affairs, or if such affairs have to be mentioned, no details are given. Paintings should be "pure" and depict landscapes, flowers, scholars, but not women or intimate situations. Clearly, the modern texts attack here strongly a popular tradition which has had a long history in China, but which became much stronger from about the sixteenth century. From this time on, novels, plays, and paintings concerned with sex began to circulate widely, in spite of all attempts of the scholars and officials to confiscate the materials and to punish the producers.

Robert van Gulik in his books [2] has made the point that the Chinese attitude toward sex changed from the time of the Manchu conquest of China. Until the early seventeenth century, sex was regarded as something "natural," and only from the seventeenth century on, was sex more and more repressed. It would seem to be worthwhile to take up this question once again by a thorough study of philosophical and half-philosophical books from Sung time on. I have the suspicion that, if there was a change, it may have begun already in Sung time. In a nineteenth century story,[3] which has strong Buddhist undertones, it is stated that in the Buddhist Tushita Heaven there are no sex relations; men and women are friends only. If, by some chance, "feelings" begin to develop between a man and a woman, the couple becomes "heavy" and sinks down to our earth, where they grow up, marry, and die in time. "Heavy" here clearly indicates "unclean," and the story is connected evidently with the Sung philosophers' speculations about the "light" versus the "heavy" or "unclean" elements producing good or bad human beings.

[2] Especially his *Sexual Life in Ancient China* (Leiden, 1961).
[3] *Yung-wan pi-chi*, 5, 9a–16b.

Social Sins

While most of the sexual sins involve harm either to another individual or to the family or to society in general, so that they might be called
"social sins," we have treated them separately because of their special
moral orientation. The rest, which is the bulk of the social sins, may be
classified as sins against other persons, and sins against the self (suicide).

The *Cheng-fa* is not too much interested in simple, straight murder
cases (grade point: 1). In this book, more attention is given to the idea
of murdering for the purpose of eating, that is, the killing of any living
beings. We remember here that animals have human souls. Killing of
animals for eating under aggravating circumstances, such as the use of
intoxicants to capture animals (punishment: hell four), is described in
detail. The text also emphasizes the punishment of persons who let
others starve or who do not let others participate in good food. Such
persons are reincarnated as "hungry spirits." Throughout the whole text,
the preoccupation with hunger and with the withholding of food is very
noteworthy—while our modern texts show this in quite a different light.

No differentiation is made for different types of suicide; whatever the
reason for taking one's own life, *Cheng-fa* reports the same punishments (grade point: 2). The modern texts differentiate clearly; there
are sinful suicides and suicides that are justified or even honorable.
For example, to kill oneself in defense of the state or the ruler or the
parents is glorious; to kill oneself in order to revenge oneself for injustice
is a light sin; and to kill oneself for trivial reasons or because of a
momentary feeling, is a more serious sin (*Yü-li:* 3). This change indicates the influence of Confucian ethics upon Buddhist thought. For a
Confucian, preservation of one's life is a basic command, but there are
cases in which other obligations are preeminent, such as serving the
father or the ruler.

Direct personal murder by different means occupied the minds of the
writers of our modern texts, and they thought up many possible cases.
But more important for them has been the atonement for creating
situations in which a person comes to death or to harm by cruelty; for
example, if officials are unnecessarily cruel to accused criminals; if jailers
cause harm to prisoners; if women beat up their servant girls, or teachers
their students; if persons get killed by the spreading of bad rumors.
Killing through wrong medicine is mentioned in all texts, but murder
caused through various magic means is more extensively discussed in the

modern texts. Much importance is given by the modern texts to unsocial attitudes causing harm to others: for example, heavy sentences to be given to persons who spread false rumors (even if no death is incurred), who love to start lawsuits, who secretly cause harm to others while on the surface they are friendly to them; to people who involve their guarantors in their debt settlements; to men who enslave girls by a contract and keep them, in violation of the contractual conditions; to people who forget their friends, or who instigate people against others, and so forth. In all these cases, the modern texts are much more detailed and discuss practically all situations causing possible tension in a Chinese village and town.

A practically new type of social sin in the modern texts are the sins against the state or the orderly structure of society. We find in the deep hells the imposters who forced emperors to abdicate or killed them; the bad officials who committed various crimes (or even murder); the rebels who did not honor their superiors; traitors; rebels; treacherous ministers or eunuchs; soldiers who murdered their officers, or who by running away involved their officers. This intrusion of nationalistic feelings into the realm of sin seems to have occurred fairly early in China. A fourteenth century text [4] already has a special section in the system of hells, the lowest of all, in which we find traitors. Here, the "classical" traitor is Ch'in K'ui,[5] the Sung minister who caused the death of Yo Fei, the patriotic general—this traitor is still proverbial today and is mentioned in our modern texts. The nineteenth century *Yung-wan pi-chi* [6] emphasizes this nationalistic aspect, and discusses a number of hells in which different categories of political traitors or criminals are punished.

Other prominent aspects of the modern texts are also related to the growth of Confucian moral thinking. We find in the hells all persons who violated any one of the other four Confucian rules, in addition to the violation of the command of "loyalty." Down to the hells go all persons violating the commandment of serving their parents; those misbehaving toward wife or husband, and those violating basic rules of "humanity." Even violations of ceremonial rules (*li*) are severely punished. The *li* are social regulations and not really religious, even if they involve the performing of ceremonies which we would regard as religious ceremonies. Yet, such violations of *li* must be punished, evidently because the *li* are one of the pillars of Confucian ethics.

[4] *Chien-teng hsien-hua*, story 6.

[5] A special study of the actions of this man and the way in which he became a symbol of "the traitor" in Chinese folklore is desirable. In general, see Henry Doré, *Recherches sur les Superstitions en Chine* (Shanghai, 1911–1938), Vol. 12, p. 1128.

[6] *Yung-wan pi-chi*, 5, 6a–9a.

Our modern texts give most detail in connection with the treatment of family members, and all transgressions of these rules are punishable sins. No acts should be done which make parents angry or sad; parents should never be forgotten, should always be fed the best food, given the best clothes; sons should always obey them; sacrifices for them should be performed. One should take care of needy clan members and orphans. Nobody should cause the breakup of a marriage; married life should be harmonious, but a husband should not listen to a wife who advises him to turn against his parents (grade point: 8). We need not mention that wives must not attempt to murder or poison their husbands (7); but also husbands should not mistreat their wives so much that their death is caused by such treatment (4). Special rules apply to the murder of brothers (5) and the custom of levirate (8). This special treatment of the levirate is interesting because in some periods of Chinese history the levirate was legally treated as a crime, while at other times it was tolerated. The *Tung-ming* regards levirate as a lack of piety (*hsiao*) and a severe sin. Cruelty against stepchildren or stepparents are also specifically mentioned (8) as violations of piety. Violations of the commandment to cultivate ties of friendship are mentioned but not stressed, and little interest is shown in the rule that one should keep harmony in the village among all citizens. But the sin (1) of inducing a young person to become a monk or nun, or to do so without serious thought, is again Confucian; basically, here Confucian familism defeated Buddhist asceticism; leaving the family is sinful for a Chinese Confucian, but a meritorious act for a real Buddhist.

In the modern texts great attention is paid also to all violations of the rules of burial. They threaten geomancers who delay the burial for selfish reasons, or citizens who cause harm to the tombs of others—a strong influence of Chinese thinking, because the concept of tomb was irrelevant for Indian Buddhists, whose corpses should be burned and not interred.

In comparison with the sexual sins, these types of social sin show perhaps even stronger changes in the direction of purely Chinese, that is mainly Confucian, values. When reading the list of these social sins in the modern texts, we feel almost nothing of true Buddhism or of Indian thought. But the stress put on sins against the parents implies clearly that family tensions were great and violations common. Why else would our texts dwell so much on the neglect of parents, even the feeding of parents, or the murder of husbands? Why must the levirate or the mistreatment of step-relatives be punished so severely, if such violations did not occur fairly often in actual life? It is perhaps significant that violations of rules of family life and the punishment of such sins is one of the favorite topics of the Chinese theater, because Chinese theater addresses itself to the middle classes, and upper-class writers and thinkers always believed that the middle and lower classes were deficient in their Confucian attitudes.

Sins Against Property

As in the case of sexual sins, property sins are a special type of social sin; they concern the material damage inflicted by the culprit on others. Since these offenses may be expected to account for a very large part of human transgressions, they are treated here as a separate group.

Old and modern texts deal very extensively with all the tricks and ways by which merchants and businessmen try to cheat their customers and to enrich themselves. The variety is great, and many details are found, from the use of false weights or counterfeit money, to the watering of rice before sale. The old texts (*Cheng-fa*) again stress the topic of food much more than do the modern texts: stealing of food or of provisions set up for travelers is mentioned specifically. On the other hand, the *Cheng-fa* already punishes bad officials who cheat the citizens when collecting taxes or other dues, who take bribes, or who give unjust sentences in courts.

In addition to all this and to special provisions for robbers, thieves, bandits, embezzlers, blackmailers, usurers, arsonists, dishonest geomancers, only the modern texts discuss irregularities occurring when brothers divide the parental property. But perhaps most significant is a fair number of sins, best described as asocial behavior, which have no parallel in the old text: the gentry should not cooperate with corrupt officials by fleecing citizens of their wealth (grade point: 8); the literati should work for public welfare and not just pretend to do so; people should not cheat in their tax payments (3), nor should officials steal grain from public granaries (3). Roads should be kept clean (3) and dead animals should not be left on the roadside (4). Traffic should not be blocked (4); canals should be kept open (4). Material from bridges or pavement bricks should not be taken away (3), nor should one steal street lanterns (3). Animals should not be kept where their dirt bothers pedestrians (3), and no farmer should let the weeds grow in his fields (3), because they would cause loss to his neighbor's fields. Some of these provisions are connected with business life, and to these should be added two prohibitions which are strongly stressed in so far as they are mentioned more than once in the same text. One should never promise to transmit a letter or message and then forget to do so (*Tung-ming:*

commitment to hells three, five, and seven—punishment several times).
One should never pursue a debtor so far that the poor victim has no way
out; if the debtor has run away, one should forget about the debt
(*Tung-ming:* grade points: 1, 6, 7). In this whole group of offenses, the
more recent texts stress much more strongly than the old text the needs
and exigencies of business life in cities, and the consideration for certain
welfare accommodations set up in cities or between cities. The ancient
Buddhists regarded the destruction of free lodging accommodations
mainly as a religious sin, because they were set up for the comfort of
pilgrims; the modern texts do not think of pilgrims, but of traveling
merchants. In general, over the last thirteen hundred years of Chinese
history, we observe that it was the Buddhists who first created and
sustained institutions of public welfare (orphanages, graveyards, hospi-
tals, traveler's accommodations, etc.), but from about the Sung period
on, the individual citizen of upper- or middle-class origin undertook such
projects, perhaps at first as a way to gain "merit," but later clearly as a
part of a social obligation.

Sins Against Religion

While, according to our previous definition, all the sexual, social, and
property sins are religious sins by virtue of their punishment in the hells,
there are, so to speak, top religious sins which are directed against
religion itself or against the gods. Often, such violations are not punished
by worldly laws, while the sins which we discussed thus far were almost
always crimes and punishable.

The old *Cheng-fa* is mainly concerned with aberrations from the
orthodox forms of Buddhism. It lists a great number of sins which are
clearly parts of the belief system or the ceremonials of non-Buddhist or
heterodox Buddhist religions or sects. None of these, however, refer to
any specifically Chinese trait. Neither a Confucian nor a Taoist custom
or belief is attacked. Most of the sins listed here refer to acts of extreme
asceticism or self-destruction, typical of Indian sects: it is sinful to state
that by burning oneself with cow dung, one will go to heaven; it is sinful
to state that by extreme penitence one will have a good fate after death,
instead of being punished for bad deeds; it is sinful to commit suicide by
drowning, in the belief that guilt is wiped out by such an act. In general,
it is sinful, according to the *Cheng-fa,* to propagate "false teachings of
body, mouth, and thought." Extreme idealism—the denying of the existence of the world—is also sinful because logically it would mean that
there can be no redemption after death. While all such sins are punished

with the sixth hell, actions aiming at the destruction of Buddhism itself are punished with treatment in hell eight. The same treatment is promised to all persons who attacked the property of religious institutions or persons or destroyed monasteries, figures, or other property of temples, of the community, or of monks. The stealing of food belonging to the deity or to monks, or taking a loan from the temple without repaying it, are similarly grave sins. Much lighter punishments (usually hell four) are meted out to persons who give wine to monks or who praise wine in the presence of monks, who ridicule monks after they had been made drunk; or to persons who induce monks in other ways to break their vows. And still lighter are the punishments for the simple breaking of vows or violations of ceremonial rules, the third group of religious sins. Finally, we have to include in this category the sins committed against animals. The *Cheng-fa* is quite outspoken on this point. The punishment for simple, purposeless killing, even for unnecessary or very cruel killing, of animals is relatively light (usually hell one). The main objects of this punishment are hunters and fishermen, with no consideration whether hunting and fishing is their only skill. Killing for the purpose of eating is punished more severely.

The modern texts show a much greater variety of sins against religion. They, too, do not attack any Confucian or Taoist practice; on the contrary, they include prominently Confucian and Taoist beliefs or practices, even folk beliefs, in their system, and turn in general against "false beliefs." Sometimes such "false beliefs" are openly named as Christian beliefs; in other cases, it seems to be some deviation from orthodox Confucian values. Also punished are people who use Western teachings and Western history—both of which presumably are felt to imply a denial of the values of Buddhism and Confucianism. A number of short stories elaborate this idea of the punishment of heterodoxy:

In one story a young servant girl who had been taught by her master about theater and about opera songs, dreamed about a visit in hell number five, where she found many of China's most famous poets of songs. A special order arrived that these poets should be transferred into the "hell in which the tongue is ploughed" as an additional punishment. They are saved only by another poet, who testified that these masters had also written serious literature of orthodox type.[7]

In a similar story a girl who studied the classics but who made a parody in classical style is brought into the hell. She sees there how heterodox scholars, who had lived almost 2,000 years ago, are still punished in the "Hell in which the tongue is pulled out" (hell four). She herself is punished with a shortened lifetime for her irreverence, and died three days before her marriage.[8]

[7] *Hsieh-to*, 12, 6b–7a.
[8] *Ibid.*, 2, 2a–3a.

In this category of false beliefs we find also persons who do not believe in gods or spirits at all. On the other hand, all references to belief systems involving ascesis, self-torture, and so forth, have disappeared in the modern texts. People are punished if they curse goblins and the gods of heaven, earth, wind, thunder, or rain; if they slander such deities or Buddhism in general, or if they simply refuse to honor them, the saints, and the holy men. Disbelief in redemption is, of course, a sin, but one which receives only very light punishment. The *Tung-ming,* with its stress upon spiritualism, threatens specifically persons who attack spiritualism, a characteristic which is missing in the *Yü-li.* New, and typically Chinese, is the stress upon religious books: it is a relatively grave sin to utter calumnies against the holy books, as well as to read such books while acting against their teaching; it is sinful to regard such teachings in the holy books as reactionary, to quote such books in order to ridicule them, and to deface religious or moralistic books. Ten times in the *Tung-ming* alone, and several times in the *Yü-li,* severe punishments are promised persons who "do not honor paper," which means printed paper. This can mean simply to throw printed paper away (instead of burning it in special ovens provided in the temples), or to step upon paper, to use it for Chinese windows (which, in earlier times, were always made of paper instead of glass), or even to use printed paper as toilet paper.[9]

The third type of sins against religion, which in many ways is indistinguishable from the social sins, has also greatly changed. We still find provisions against drinking, enlarged by provisions against smoking and gambling—both popular Chinese customs—as well as against breaking of religious vows. But the main stress is laid upon acts which violate, not provisions of Buddhism, but those of Confucianism. Here we find the threat of harsh punishment for all persons who violate the fundamental Confucian commandments in aspects which are not per se punished by worldly law: those who do not show piety (*hsiao*) toward parents, or friendliness (*ti*) toward brothers; wives who do not obey their husbands and their husbands' parents; students who do not honor and obey their teachers. This stress upon the values of the family and upon Confucianism in general is much stronger than the stress upon clearly Buddhist or even clearly Taoist values. We can safely assume that the protection of printed paper and the holy books refers more to Confucian writings than

---

[9] The use of toilet paper seems to be quite old in China, perhaps as old as T'ang time, but special studies are not yet made. It appears that before the use of paper or cloth (for this see *Mo-yü-lu,* 1, 12b, with an early reference), wooden plates or bricks were used. Discussion of these plates and bricks, which were locally still used in Ming times, in *Chia-i sheng-yen,* edition *Li-tai hsiao-shuo pi-chi hsüan,* Ming, I, 98–99.

to strictly religious writings. And, significantly, while in general the punishments of sins against religion are, in the modern texts, much lighter than in the *Cheng-fa,* in the group of violations of familial values the punishments are extremely severe.

The sins against animals are more elaborated in the *Tung-ming* than in the *Yü-li.* And punishments again are in general more severe than in the *Cheng-fa.* For instance, people who catch birds in nets are punished first in hell two, then in five, and then in one of four sub-hells of hell nine.[10] Special sins are the following: poisoning of fish (hells two, five, and four sections in nine); hunting by means of laying traps, a method by which many animals, even those that cannot be eaten, are killed (hell seven); simple burning down of forests in mountains; [11] digging out the holes of animals; collecting eggs or unborn animals; slaughtering of cows and dogs; or eating of meat of cows, dogs, or meat in general. This strong stress upon the protection of animals is interesting. Several points should be kept in mind in this connection. Chinese Buddhist texts, as we have stated above, make it clear that it is not the animal body that deserves protection, since an animal is a human being changed into animal form as a part of a punishment for former sins. Killing an animal is, therefore, like killing a human being and must be prohibited. But here begins the dilemma: while no one should kill an animal, the main point of being condemned to live as an animal is the eventual death under the hands of a butcher or a hunter. This quasi-certainty of painful and violent death makes life in animal form a dreadful punishment. There must be persons who violate Buddhist law by killing animals, because otherwise the most punitive end of the reincarnation in animal form would never occur. Buddhism has not really resolved this dilemma. It was in no country ever the religion of all citizens, and in several Buddhist countries Buddhists ate and still eat meat if the animal it comes from has been slaughtered by a non-Buddhist. In the same temples in which we find our *shan-shu,* with their condemnation of killing of animals, the believers bring heads of pigs and whole chickens as sacrifices, because meat is the most delicious and yet most costly and rare dish, and gods certainly like a costly sacrifice more than a cheap one. Moreover, the believer can eat the sacrifice after the deity has eaten the spiritual "essence" of the sacrifice. Several times in history, Chinese governments have forbidden, not the slaughtering of all animals, but at

[10] The numbers should be lowered by one each, here and in the following sentences, to make them comparable to the numbers in the *Cheng-fa.* See the explanation in the beginning of this chapter.

[11] In the *Cheng-fa* it is clear that the prohibition against burning down mountain forests is mainly in order to prevent damage to monastic or temple properties; in the modern texts the main stress is on prevention of the death of animals.

least the slaughtering of cows, because for Buddhists the cow is the foremost animal, though not a sacred animal as it is for Hindus. The laws against slaughtering of cows have been observed much more strictly in Japan, where meat (excluding fish, which is not counted as meat) has almost diappeared from the menu. In China, ordinary citizens have little occasion to commit sins against animals, because in their poverty they eat meat only a few times a year and very little meat at that.

Note, however, that only the killing of animals is punishable and sinful. To beat animals, to mistreat them, to let them suffer hunger or die of starvation is not a sin. It is, so to say, a part of the condition of animal life. Thus, the Chinese have not created "societies for the prevention of cruelty to animals." On the other hand, it is logical that animals with personal souls may commit crimes against the law and may be punished by a process of law. For instance, a regulation of 737 A.D.[12] stated that if animals gore people, their horns should be cut off; if they bite, their ears should be cut off, and if they kick, their legs should be fettered. This attitude, however, is neither typically Buddhist, nor limited to countries like China.

On the other hand, if a wild beast attacks and kills people, it may act upon a clear permission from a deity and, in such a case, should not be regarded as punishable. A story from the late nineteenth century illustrates the point:

When a man went to the toilet during the night, he heard a voice saying: "I have not had anything to eat for three days. But now the god allowed me to eat a bride in the village such and such. Thus, I will have no more hunger." The man found out that the speaker and his friend were both wolves, and as the family was blood-related to his own family, he went over and warned them. In the morning, the mother gathered firewood instead of the girl whose normal duty this was. A wolf came, ran the mother down, entered the house, and took the girl. When people tried to pursue the wolf, other wolves arrived and the hungry wolf got his food in spite of all precautions.[13]

In addition to the protection of animals against being killed, the modern texts have severe and repeated punishments for persons who "do not honor the five kinds of grain," that is, mainly for persons who consciously or unintentionally step on grain or who throw food away. Even sitting on grain is punished by treatment in hells six and seven. This idea is absent from the *Cheng-fa,* although this old text has such a preoccupation with hunger. It seems to be typically Chinese, and is a motif which is found not rarely in Chinese folktales. It may reflect the constant threat of hunger which, in China, meant lack of wheat or other

[12] Noboru Niida, *T'ang Law* (Tokyo, 1933), p. 856.
[13] *Erh-ju,* 2, 2b–3a.

grains rather than absence of meat or vegetables. Comparing the changes in the attitude toward sins against basic commandments of religion, we observe that sins involving the violation of religious buildings or the property of religious institutions have lost their importance. Sins against religion in general focus upon Christianity and atheism or skepticism rather than upon ascetic deviations.

In modern times, all deities, whether Buddhist or Taoist, or other deities of the mixed folk religion, are acceptable. Violations of specifically Buddhist rules are much less important in comparison with violations of the basic commandments of Chinese Confucianism. In other words, violations of rules tending to protect society, and especially the narrow circle of family and relations, are, in the modern books on sins, taken much more seriously than violations of points of the dogma, or of property belonging to deities or priests.

The priests themselves do not fare well in the modern texts. The old *Cheng-fa* is full of details of sins by people against monks or nuns. The modern texts talk almost exclusively of sins committed by monks or nuns. In folklore and in Chinese theater, the monk is more often than not a sinful person who attempts to seduce women or plans intrigues.

CHAPTER FOUR

A Note on Sin, Guilt, and Sex

Psychoanalytical psychology sees the origin of the feeling of guilt in the Oedipus complex, resulting from conscious or unconscious, although repressed, sexual attraction between mother and son, or father and daughter, leading to hostility, particularly between father and son, which reinforces the feeling of guilt. Sexual inhibitions and fears have been regarded as a corollary to this complex. A recent comparative study [1] has tried to show, with a quantitative method, that societies observing a strict postpartum sex taboo (i.e., societies with a so-called "diluted marriage complex") tend to be also societies with a high percentage of polygynous marriages and a high percentage of mother-child households. According to that study, such societies have a strongly developed Oedipus complex. The study did not include Chinese society, and some of its premises are difficult to establish for China. There were polygynous marriages in China, but in the absence of reliable statistics we cannot say whether Chinese polygyny can be regarded as "high" (i.e., whether at least 40 percent of all married women were polygynous).[2] Mother-child households did exist in China, but seem to have been rare at all times. Postpartum sex taboos in China would put China in the category of societies with a short taboo period.[3] Modern as well as old texts state that there should be no intercourse from the sixth month of pregnancy to the end of the second month after childbirth.[4] If the Chinese seem to be low in all these points, according to the theory of the aforementioned

---

[1] William N. Stephens, *The Oedipus Complex: Cross-cultural Evidence* (Glencoe, 1962), pp. 2, 3, and 7.

[2] *Ibid.*, p. 5. All information seems to indicate that there was a low frequency of polygyny in China.

[3] *Ibid.*, p. 4. The period is defined as long if it lasts at least a year.

[4] Lu Lou-sha, *Hsing-yü t'ao-lun ta-kuan* (Shanghai, 1926), p. 19. I wish to express my thanks to the Institute for Sex Research, Indiana University, Bloomington, which allowed me to read this and other Chinese texts on sexual matters in their library. Inez de Beauclair (*Bulletin of the Institute of Ethnology*, Vol. 10 [1960], p. 175, note) reports from Kuangtung province that intercourse is regarded as harmful from the fifth month of pregnancy to the hundredth day after childbirth.

study one should then expect few sexual inhibitions and fears and a low level of guilt feelings.

The question of sexual attraction between son and mother is completely tabooed in Chinese literature. Incestual fantasies of such type would be regarded as so immoral that no writer would dare to talk about them. I have the feeling that it would be difficult to find even unconscious allusions in Chinese writings.[5] In contrast, the love between father and son is a predominant ethical precept, so much so that even a hint of difficulties in the relation between father and son would be regarded as improper. Thus, I believe that on the basis of literary documents these points can be neither proved nor disproved. From the absence of relevant statements in the literature one can obviously not conclude that there was no attraction between sons and mothers and no hostility between fathers and sons in China.

Fortunately, the question of sexual inhibitions lends itself more easily to literary study. A text like the following is typical:

Only (the relation between) husband and wife is proper. It cannot even be compared with illicit love. Though (people) speak of a "heavenly union" the reason (for intercourse) is the continuation of the line of ancestors.[6] But a couple should control its sexual urge. Only if the sexual urge is restrained does it create good luck.[7] Without restraint, it is mere debauchery. Then, taboo days will be violated, deities and spirits will get angry. Pay attention to the taboo days (when no intercourse should take place): the san-yüan [8] and wu-la,[9] the birthdays of deities and saints; in addition, the day of mother's trouble,[10] the birthdays and days of the death of the parents.[11] There are the four separations [12] and the four breaks,[13] the crossing of heaven and earth,[14] the nine poisonous days [15] and the days of amnesty,[16] also the first and the

[5] A collection of over 800 Chinese dreams which I am analyzing shows, however, the great emotional attachment of sons and daughters to their mother and the emotional distance from their father.

[6] And not pleasure.

[7] A Chinese proverb states: "To take medicine for a thousand days is not as good as to sleep alone for one night" (quoted in Neng-kai-chai man-lu, 5, 20a).

[8] According to the old calendar, the fifteenth day of the first, seventh, and tenth months (Henry Doré, Recherches sur les Superstitions en Chine [Shanghai, 1911–1938], Vol. 6, p. 17). A note after this chapter recommends that one should look the date up in the calendar.

[9] Five special days; the note says one should look them up in the calendar.

[10] Apparently one's own birthday.

[11] This refers not only to the days of the deaths of the parents. Intercourse during the period of mourning for the parents (27 months) was also forbidden (Li-chi, Sang ta-chi, 2, 20; Couvreur translation, Vol. 2, p. 241).

[12] One day before each equinox and solstice.

[13] One day before the beginning of each of the four seasons.

[14] According to a note, this refers to the fifteenth day of the fifth month.

[15] According to a note, this means the fifth to the seventh, the fifteenth to the seventeenth, and the twenty-fifth to the twenty-seventh days of the fifth month.

[16] No note given.

fifteenth days of the month. One should note also the birthdays of ancestors. Furthermore, the *keng-shen* and *chia-tse* days,[17] and in each of the four seasons and of the eight sectors of the year, all *ping* and *ting* days.[18] Furthermore, days of great cold and heat, of great wind and rain, of earthquake, thunder and lightning, during eclipses of the sun and the moon [19] and under the light of the sun,[20] the moon or the planets; (one should not have intercourse) near the well, the hearth, coffins and tombs, not during drunkenness and after one has eaten too much, nor when one is very angry or depressed or in fear; also not when one has been on a distant trip or when one is tired; nor when one is not clean after a trip and not directly after an illness. All these (rules) are ways to preserve the body and for a pious son the prime rules to keep his body intact. Whoever does not follow these taboos, has his lifetime shortened.[21]

We have a fairly great number of texts, many earlier than this one, which contain the same or almost the same rules. They are so complex that printed lists existed which were sold on the streets and contained the days which were allowed for intercourse.[22] A few additional remarks from fairly early texts elucidate the sexual fears and taboos of Chinese even further. A seventeenth century text states that although menstruation begins with the fourteenth year and a man becomes fertile in his sixteenth year, men should marry when thirty and women when twenty; but "today" people marry too early:

Therefore, there are no pregnancies in spite of intercourse; or if a pregnancy occurs, the babies are not born alive; or if they are born alive, they often do not live long. Therefore, the men of old times all became over a hundred years old and were not decrepit. They knew the *tao*.[23] Today, people marry

[17] The fifty-seventh day of the 60-day cycle and the first day of this cycle.

[18] The four seasons are the 15-day periods in which the four seasons begin; the eight sectors are these four seasons and the four 15-day periods in which the equinoxes and solstices are. *Ping* and *ting* days are the third and fourth days in 10-day periods, connected with the element fire, the male element.

[19] Already the *Hsü Po-wu-chih,* 2, 1b, mentions that children begotten during eclipses will be often sick, and children begotten at the time of new moon, full moon, and half moon, will be stupid. Some authors recommend a hundred days of abstinence, others two hundred days of chastity from the ninth month on, when it becomes cold, in order to avoid sickness in Spring and to remain young and vigorous (*Yü-li (chih) pao ch'ao,* p. 108).

[20] Darkness seems to have been a condition for intercourse since a long time. The *Tso-chuan* (quoted by Robert van Gulik, *Sexual Life in Ancient China* [Leiden, 1961], p. 34) already states that intercourse should take place during the night. A modern text forbids intercourse when candles are lighted, and at dawn, and asks the partners to close their eyes (*Yü-fang pi-chüeh*).

[21] *Hsing-shan fu-pao p'ien,* p. 37a. The edition used was printed shortly after 1875. Earlier texts, such as the *Yü-fang pi-chüeh* and the *Su-nü-ching,* have even larger lists of taboo days than this text.

[22] Lu Lou-sha, p. 22.

[23] The heavenly principle.

too early, they are decrepit before they are fifty, and people of seventy are quite rare.[24]

The same writer mentions three categories of reasons for infertility even when the marriage did not begin too early in life: (1) there exists lack of virtue of the ancestors, bad personal behavior, or defects in one's own heart; (2) the man's *yang*[25] is not strong enough to produce any development;[26] (3) the blood of the wife or concubine is too cold and cannot accept pregnancy. He then continues:

If you ask how this can be remedied, I say: "This is not difficult. Only repent your actions in life, eliminate all transgressions[27] and evil deeds. . . . If one has done good deeds long enough, then automatically he receives luck and rewards from heaven. Merit does not mean to repair or build Buddhist or Taoist temples or to read canonical books or to recite Buddha."[28]

Following a general tradition, another text recommends that a pregnant woman should always behave correctly, live in a quiet room, live in harmony, speak only good words; people should read to her parts of the Books of Odes and the Book of Documents and talk about ceremonial behavior[29] so that she will get a good child. Even twentieth century Chinese sex books (and similar Japanese books) enumerate restrictions upon sexual relations which are not astrological, as are many of the restrictions in the older books, but which retain many of the older restrictions. For example, there is only one good position for intercourse, namely, that the woman lies flat on her back;[30] intercourse in the tenth month and the first half of the eleventh month of the year is best; during spring, intercourse is not good, in the fifth month of the year it is permissible, in the eighth month much better;[31] intercourse during the day is bad;[32] and between 1 and 2 A.M. or in the early morning it is harmful.

---

[24] *Chi-szu chen-pao,* pp. 1a–2a, printed in the *Shê-sheng tsung-yao,* compiled by Hung Chu-yo, reprint of a 1638 edition, Institute for Sex Research Library (see n. 4 above).

[25] Male principle.

[26] *Hua,* i.e., impregnation.

[27] This is the term used for lighter sins.

[28] *Chi-szu chen-pao,* p. 3a.

[29] *Chung-tse pi-p'ou,* in the *Chi-szu chen-pao,* p. 8b. This text, too, has all the prohibited days for sexual intercourse, similar to the book mentioned above (see n.24).

[30] Lu Lou-sha, p. 20. This is also indicated in *Tung-hsüan-tse* (van Gulik, *Sexual Life,* p. 126), although this text describes thirty different positions. The reason for the "normal" position seems to be that the man/male/heaven has to be above the woman/female/earth. The alchemistic text *Ts'an t'ung ch'i* (sec. 56; see *Isis,* Vol. 53, p. 254) also recommends this position.

[31] Lu Lou-sha, p. 21.

[32] A text reports with all signs of disapproval that the Yao tribes in South China have intercourse during the day in the forests, completely naked (*Ch'iu-yü-wan*

The best time to have intercourse is three hours after dinner, between 10 and 12 P.M., after having had one or two hours of sleep.[33] No intercourse should occur when one is drunk, or at the beginning of menstruation,[34] when one is nervous, tired, exhausted, if one of the partners is not willing, during times of strong emotions, and when there is any illness, especially any sexual disease.[35] A modern Japanese authority recommends two intercourses per week for persons of twenty years of age, one for persons between thirty and forty; one intercourse per month between forty and fifty. At fifty one should not have sexual relations or, if the man is very strong, very occasionally only.[36] But in any case, more than one intercourse in one night is regarded as harmful.[37] If one had to keep all these rules constantly in mind and had to be afraid that in any

sui-pi, 2, 24b). The author seems to object against the time and the nakedness. All texts mention the "colored candles" in the bridal room; modern movies, too, show them. This indicates that during the initial love play, complete darkness was not regarded as necessary. The reason seems to be that a man should not see the female organs. If a man, for instance, sees the sexual organs of his wife in his dreams, this indicates fights (Chou-kung chieh-meng). In a nineteenth century story, a man who visited a foreign prostitute for the first time was shocked when the girl undressed immediately and completely. He saw that her sexual organ was hairy and this shocked him so much that the evening was lost (Erh-ju, 2, 8b). A woman should have no pubic hair (Su-nü-ching, p. 21), or at least not much (Yü-fang pi-chüeh). On the other hand, the myth about the discovery of sex life presupposes looking at the sexual organs: primeval men were naked and observed that men had an excrescence, while women had a cavity. Thus they invented the intercourse (Ch'ih p'o-tse chuan).

[33] Su-nü-ching, p. 20.

[34] In order to beget a child, one should have intercourse three and a half days after the end of menstruation (Su-nü-ching, p. 20). The Chung-tse pi-p'ou (pp. 6a and 8a) says that after the sixth day after menstruation a woman does not conceive any more and should not be allowed to have intercourse because this would reduce her fertility. Lu Lou-sha, p. 21, recommends the period between the seventh and fourteenth days after menstruation as good days. I assume that he means after the beginning of menstruation. In both cases, these remarks indicate that the "rhythm system" was known in China since many generations.

[35] Mentioned by Lu Lou-sha, p. 21.

[36] Chinese texts are a bit more generous. Yüan Mei (Hsü Tse-pu-yü, 8, quoted by P'an Kuang-tan, Hsing-hsin-li hsüeh, p. 326, note 93) says that men can have sex life from sixteen to sixty-four. The Su-nü-ching (p. 18) makes a difference between intercourse and ejaculation: strong men up to thirty years of age can have intercourse twice a day; up to forty, once; up to fifty, every fifth day; up to sixty, every tenth day, and after seventy, once a month. But ejaculation should happen only once every four days with men below thirty, and so forth. The Yü-fang pi-chüeh allows this to happen once every two days. Both texts forbid ejaculation after age sixty. Other texts recommend for commoners and even for the ruler intercourse once every five days up to age fifty (Yeh-k'o ts'ung-shu, 16, 5a, and 29, 1a). Moreover, one should not have intercourse with women over forty (Yü-fang pi-chüeh).

[37] Lu Lou-sha, p. 23. In a story it is reported that a man died because he had three ejaculations during one night. This caused too much "cold" in his organs (Leng-lu tsa-chih, 4, 1b).

case of violation either his health would be destroyed, or miscarriages would occur, or children with bad character qualities would be born, or the deities would be offended and mete out punishments, Chinese sex life could not have been very "natural," and sexual inhibitions and fears must have been quite strong from fairly early medieval times down to the present. One might here make the intriguing point (which we cannot, of course, even attempt to prove) that these sexual inhibitions and fears might have played an appreciable role in the control of population growth.[38] This would mean that with the disappearance of "popular superstitions" and their replacement with "scientific attitudes" these controls disappeared, and thus China's "population explosion" was even intensified.

It is to be hoped that these remarks, together with the other material on sexual sin and guilt in general in this book, will serve to stimulate a new investigation of the theories of and around the Oedipus complex.

[38] P'an Kuang-tan, *op. cit.,* p. 325, note 79, calculated that only a hundred days in a year were auspicious for sexual relations.

CHAPTER FIVE

Scholars Evaluate Sin and Shame

Sin in a Selected Group of Short Stories

Thus far, we have analyzed a type of literature which in only a few exceptional cases was composed by common, relatively uneducated people. Most of it was written by men with some education for the consumption and education of the common man. We had reason to assume that every Chinese was, to some degree, exposed to this kind of indoctrination. This literature, which serves to instill and to maintain certain "motives and predispositions" among the lower classes, shows the tremendous stress which is laid upon the concepts of guilt and sin as guiding principles of social behavior.

As many Chinese scholars looked down upon these books as superstitious and trivial, we could expect that scholars had a different value-system in which guilt did not play a role, or played a different role. This expectation is the more justified as we have at least one area in which the values of the elite differ widely from the values which are used to indoctrinate the common man: the attitudes toward war. While the Confucianist writings and Chinese philosophy in general regard all military activities as undesirable, though sometimes necessary, the material written for the common man, and apparently also the material written *by* common men, extols war, fighting, and heroism.

With the shift from literature for the uneducated to literature for the educated, our method changes. We separated, out of a collection of more than fifteen hundred short stories, all those in which acts were mentioned that the writer regarded as bad, which either offered an evaluation of the act or reported a punishment. We deduced, thus, from the reported behavior of individuals the principal motives or predispositions, but instead of using our own standards, we used the moral standards of the evaluating Chinese author. The texts come from different periods, but they are not evenly distributed over the centuries. Almost 50 percent are from the eighteenth century. They were originally collected for a different purpose,[1] and contain in addition to what normally would be called "short stories," also some "pen notes" (*pi-chi*) from the fourteenth century, some abstracts of theater plays (nineteenth century) and some recently published modern folktales (twentieth century). Such a collection can in no way be regarded either as a random sample or as a "representative selection." Considering the size and diversity of Chinese literature, and its spread over time, it seems to me to be futile or impossible to attempt setting up such samples. Any conclusions drawn on the basis of this material should therefore be taken with caution: they are valid for our material, but may or may not be valid for "Chinese literature in general."

In this collection, we found 172 texts containing "bad" actions (i.e. in 11 percent of all stories). Our first observation was the complete absence of precisely the same sins and punishments reported in the *shan-shu*. All stories were much more vague in these respects. Besides, punishment for an offense was not always meted out by fate or by the court of the hells, but was often given immediately, on earth, by supernatural beings (deities, spirits, deified animals) or even by human beings (see Table 4). Punishment by human beings was in most cases ordered by a judge in the course of a trial, but there were cases in which ordinary persons meted out the deserved punishment to the criminal or sinner, either in form of personal acts of revenge or otherwise, consciously or unconsciously. Sins of a directly religious character were, as was to be expected, punished more often by fate or by the god of hell, while offenses involving physical violence, that is, social sins, remained more often in the hands of human judges. However, it was interesting that

---

[1] All the selections which were analyzed in the book *Die chinesische Novelle* (*Artibus Asiae,* Supplement No. 9, Ascona, 1948), about a thousand short stories, have been used. Full source references will be found in that book. To these were added 26 theater plays reported by Wilhelm Grube, *Pekinger Volkskunde;* 122 modern folktales from various modern publications, all of which have been used in my *Typen chinesischer Volksmärchen* (Helsinki, 1937); all stories in the fourteenth century collections *Chien-teng hsien-hua* (21) and *Shan-chü hsin-hua* (151); 28 early Ming period stories (none of these occurs in the selection used in this chapter); 107 stories from chapters 4–6 of the nineteenth century collection *Yung-wan pi-chi;* 3 stories from the eighteenth century *Ti-kung-an;* and one story each from the very early *Sou-chen hou-chi* and *Shu-i-chi.* The distribution in the 1574 story collection is as follows: 4.6 percent from before 1000 A.D.; 10.9 percent from the fourteenth century; 1.7 percent from the fifteenth and sixteenth; 4.3 percent from the seventeenth; 49.4 percent from the eighteenth; 21.4 percent from the nineteenth; and 7.8 percent from the twentieth century.

TABLE 4

THE PUNISHING AGENCY IN 172 SHORT STORIES

Punishing agency:	Human	Supernatural	Fate or god of hell	?
Type of offense:				
Violence	40.3[a] (27)[b]	22.4 (15)	34.3 (23)	3.0 (2)
Sexual	40.9 (18)	20.5 (9)	38.6 (17)	—
Property	28.9 (11)	18.4 (7)	42.1 (16)	10.5 (4)
Religious	13.1 (3)	21.7 (5)	65.2 (15)	—
Total averages	34.3 (59)	20.9 (36)	41.3 (71)	3.5 (6)

[a] Figures expressed in percentages.
[b] Figures in parentheses are actual numbers.

sexual crimes, too, were more often punished by human law than by fate. From the *shan-shu* we would have expected that sins of this type would evoke strong interference by the powers of heavenly justice.

If we study the social class of the sinner or lawbreaker (Table 5), we

TABLE 5

THE SOCIAL CLASS OF THE CULPRIT IN 172 SHORT STORIES

Social class:	Upper	Middle	Lower	Unknown or not relevant (left out) number of cases
Type of offense:				
Violence	48.4[a] (30)[b]	30.6 (19)	21.0 (13)[c]	(5)
Sexual	44.8 (17)	39.5 (15)	15.7 (6)	(6)
Property	37.8 (14)	37.8 (14)	24.4 (9)	(1)
Religious	54.6 (12)	36.4 (8)	9.0 (2)	(1)
Total average	45.9 (73)	35.2 (56)	18.9 (30)	7.6 (13)

[a] Figures expressed in percentages.
[b] Figures in parentheses are actual numbers.
[c] All crimes for the three classes total 100 percent.

find that the authors ascribed fewer offenses of violence and more sexual sins to middle-class people than to others, while they attributed few religious and many property sins to the lower class. Impressions gained from general reading of Chinese materials would have led us to the same conclusions. In Table 5 we defined the "upper class" as landlords, officials, and scholars, "middle class" as merchants, craftsmen, artisans, folk doctors, geomancers, ordinary priests and nuns, and as "lower class" all farmers and other rural people, together with servants and slaves, beggars and other urban poor. It is perhaps significant that the women are more often involved in sexual sins than in any other type (Table 6). This may reflect a belief, also visible in the *shan-shu,* that

TABLE 6

SEX OF THE CULPRIT IN 172 SHORT STORIES

Type of offense		Female
Violence		7.5[a] (5)[b]
Sexual		13.7 (6)
Property		2.6 (1)
Religious		8.7 (2)
	Total average	8.1 (14)

[a] Figures expressed in percentages.
[b] Figures in parentheses are actual numbers.

women are mainly interested in sex and are, basically, the seducers, though such a belief might reflect male wishful thinking rather than actual conditions. After all, all the stories in our selection were written by men. As far as I can see, from the eighteenth century on, writers began to think more seriously about female sex life. Let me give two short stories which are not in our collection:

A young mother became a widow at seventeen years of age; she remained unmarried to her death, and this meant a great honor for her clan. But shortly before her death she called the family and told them that they should never force a widow to remain chaste. When the family was startled to hear this, she told them that as a young widow she once fell in love with a man in the next room. Her desire grew so much that several times she walked toward the other room. One night, after a final victory over her desires, she visited the other room in a dream. The moment she climbed into the bed of her idol, she saw on the bed, not him, but her dead husband with blood on his face and crying. Immediately she woke up in horror and heard her baby cry. Since then, the author says, there were many chaste widows in this clan, also some who remarried, but there was never any scandal.[2]

Since the thirteenth century, remarriage of widows was abhorred by the upper class, although it occurred in the other classes. And no earlier writer seems to have thought about what this rule might have meant for the unfortunate women.

[2] *Hsieh-to,* 9, 4b–5a.

In the other story,[3] a chaste girl is miraculously saved by the goddess Kuan-yin during the flood of 1788. She is brought into a temple with pedestals on the one side for wise women, on the other side for chaste women. She finds her own place here and is deified. She later told her brother of this in a vision and informed him that chastity in women is as important as honor in men. In this story, the author introduces the new concept that a woman who remains chaste deserves the same honors by religion as an honest and patriotic man normally receives by religion. It is only in the early nineteenth century that the whole question of equality of women is taken up as a broad and vital issue.

We attempted to find out whether our material, covering, as it does, several centuries, would show any significant shifts, especially an increase in sexual sins or a decrease in transgressions of a more narrowly defined religious character. But no change could be detected.

In Chinese literature some so-called "character traits" of Chinese from different parts of China have been mentioned. A special study of such "regional prejudices" is now under way.[4] Our Table 7 shows that

TABLE 7

REGIONAL DISTRIBUTION OF CULPRITS IN 172 SHORT STORIES

Area:	North China	Central China	South China	?
Types of offense:				
Violence	52.3[a] (35)[b]	32.9 (22)	4.4 (3)	10.5 (7)
Sexual	45.5 (20)	38.7 (17)	4.4 (2)	11.4 (5)
Property	60.6 (23)	21.1 (8)	7.9 (3)	10.5 (4)
Religious	43.5 (10)	39.1 (9)	8.7 (2)	8.7 (2)
Total average	51.2 (88)	32.6 (56)	5.8 (10)	10.5 (18)

[a] Figures expressed in percentages.
[b] Figures in parentheses are actual numbers.

religious and sexual sins were relatively more common in Central China, while offenses involving property were more often mentioned for North China. We would, impressionistically, have expected more sexual offenses in Central and South China and more offenses involving violence in North China.

If we put our question in a different way by hypothesizing that a belief in a punishment by human agencies alone would indicate a higher degree

[3] *Ibid.*, 12, 5b–6a.
[4] "Chinese Regional Stereotypes," in *Asian Survey*, Vol. 5 (1965), No. 12, pp. 596–608.

of rationality, we might expect, first, differences between different parts of China because, in the centuries for which we have the best documentation, Central China was regarded as "more progressive" than, for instance, North China; and secondly, we might expect differences between different social classes, because the upper class often is regarded as more rational than the other classes. However, an analysis of our material showed no regional differences of this kind. Class differences, on the other hand, seemed to be of some importance. Contrary to our expectation, the crimes of upper-class members, reported in our texts, were much less often punished by human courts, and crimes of the middle and lower classes much more often than we expected (Table 8).

TABLE 8

REGIONAL AND CLASS ATTITUDES TOWARD
PUNISHMENT OF SINS [a]

Punishing agency:	Human beings	Supernatural beings	Fate or god of hell	Average
Area:				
North China	55.4[b] (31)[c]	60.6 (20)	56.4 (35)	57.0
Central China	35.7 (20)	33.3 (11)	40.3 (25)	37.0
South China	9.0 (5)	6.1 (2)	3.3 (2)	6.0
	100.1 (56)	100.0 (33)	100.0 (62)	100.0 (151)
Class:				
Upper	20.0 (11)	60.6 (20)	59.7 (40)	45.8
Middle	54.6 (30)	24.2 (8)	26.9 (18)	36.1
Lower	25.5 (14)	15.2 (5)	13.4 (9)	18.1
	100.1 (55)	100.0 (33)	100.0 (67)	100.0 (155)

[a] Cases in which area or class were not known or not relevant were left out: 10.1 percent of regional cases; 7.7 percent of class cases.
[b] Figures expressed in percentages.
[c] Figures in parentheses are actual numbers.

It sounds like a paradox, that in having upper-class people punished more often by supernatural powers, the authors were probably trying to be realistic, since it was not a secret that in real life the members of the upper class often found ways to cover up their crimes and thus avoid trial and punishment by courts. What the writers evidently wished to show was that such persons would receive their punishment by higher

elements, by supernatural beings, fate, or the god of hell, all of which are impartial and incorruptible. They did not wish to indicate that members of the upper class were more fervent believers in supernatural redemption.

In general, the literati-authors of our stories were not specifically interested in sin or guilt. They mentioned various kinds of sins or offenses, whatever they found interesting or extraordinary, which is the privilege of a novelist. Offenses involving physical violence occurred more frequently (38.8 percent) than violations of religious rules or crimes against supernatural beings (13.4 percent), and sexual sins (25.6 percent) more than theft, that is, property sins (22.1 percent). It is true that only in about one-third of the cases was the punishment meted out by human justice, but punishment by nonhuman agencies, as mentioned in these stories, did not follow closely the rules set up by the *shan-shu*. In general, punishments set up by the *shan-shu* are much harsher, much more cruel than the punishments which the sinners received in the stories.

Shame in a Selected Group of Short Stories

The collection of more than 1,500 short stories, which was used for a discussion of the literary treatment of morally bad, that is, sinful, actions, yielded little information on the subject of shame. There were only sixteen clear cases—cases in which the Chinese author indicated that shame was involved, not cases in which we as outsiders would assume that shame was felt. In other words, roughly 1 percent of all stories dealt with shame. Therefore, another 250 short stories, mainly of the eighteenth and nineteenth centuries [5] were scrutinized and we arrived at a total of thirty-four cases of shame in a new total of over 1,600 stories. Two percent of all stories dealt with shame, enough, I believe, to show the basic types.

As in the case of the treatment of bad actions, the authors write as if the events they describe had really happened. We can, in a very few cases, prove that they did happen in more or less the way the writers described them. Other stories are, in the eyes of a modern observer, clearly fantasies. Perhaps the author felt the same way; perhaps he really believed in miracles and magic. But in any case, he evaluates the case as he would evaluate a true report, and we are interested in such an evaluation of social interactions.

[5] In fact, this is the same set of stories which has been used in chapter vi, Suicide in Short Stories. See note 1 of chapter vi.

The cases involving shame can be divided into three groups. The first, of sixteen stories, deals with actions that the *shan-shu* would definitely regard as sinful acts. Often, the actions have a sexual character. For example, being seen undressed is, for a woman, a sin which could be condoned only if the man who saw her was her husband or became her husband immediately, or if it happens for the purpose of an act of piety. In all these cases, the culprit and his family are exposed to shame because the sinful act had or might become publicly known. It must be emphasized that anyhow the individual receives punishment in hell for this act. Thus, in all these cases, shame is an additional punishment.

We know from the *shan-shu* that sinful acts are punishable even if they are not done on purpose or knowingly. Persons caught in such situations feel ashamed when and because their action becomes publicly known. Such situations were assigned to the second group of cases of shame, together with cases in which someone suspected of having committed a sin has no way of proving his innocence. This group, then, comprises cases that are tragic in the classical sense. One might say that the decisive motif in all such cases is *suspicion*. For example, when a woman was raped, even if she resisted and was killed, the suspicion remains that she may have had some sort of forbidden relation with the rapist before the act and that, therefore, she was not completely innocent. But the Chinese moralist typically does not make use of psychological deliberations of this kind; he simply takes a formalistic view: a raped woman is a woman who had illicit relations, and this is sinful whatever the circumstances. In both these two groups of cases of shame, the sexual element is obvious, and a considerable number of cases involve women.

The third set, eleven cases, however, is limited exclusively to men,[6] and no sin is involved, even though in several cases it is a woman who shames the man. In these cases, in which the conceit and ignorance of men in high positions is publicly exposed, the social status of the man is attacked, though he does not lose his status legally. Most of the stories in this third group can be regarded as jokes; they are not serious, at least not when compared to the other cases. Shame here is solely the result of making a certain behavior trait publicly known; the trait as such is not sinful, and no punishment would occur in the other world if the actions had remained secret. All cases of this third class, incidentally, involve men of high class or at least of great wealth and status, while in the other cases, the actors belong to different classes. Our material is too slight to

---

[6] In this category, only one case was found in the collection of short stories first used. All the other ten cases are from the 250 newly added stories. This was one of the main reasons to add stories to the original set.

attempt any further analysis, for example as to changes over time [7] or to regional differences; in fact it appears doubtful whether even a much larger set of data would yield more results on shame. We probably have to accept the fact that short-story writers down to the twentieth century were not much interested in shame. When they did talk about it, shame was usually a side element in a story of guilt and sin unless the whole story was more or less a joke. It remains to be seen whether one may draw the conclusion that the importance of shame and shaming in Chinese society has been overrated.

TREATMENT OF SHAME IN SHORT STORIES

An Exposure or Potential Exposure of Sinful Acts Committed in Secrecy—(1) Tu Mu-chih, a scholar, told a lie relating to sex affairs. He was exposed as a liar in public (E. D. Edwards, *Chinese Prose Literature,* Vol. 2, pp. 175–177). (2) Chuang-tse's widow, wanting to help her supposedly sick lover, opened her husband's coffin in order to take out his brain as a medicine. Chuang-tse was not dead and exposed her unfaithfulness. She committed suicide (*Chin-ku ch'i-kuan,* Text 20). (3) Chu Mai-ch'en's wife divorced him because of his poverty and married a rich man. When Chu got a high position, she felt sorry. He shamed her publicly, so that she committed suicide (*Chin-ku ch'i-kuan,* Text 32a).[8]

(4) Mr. Lu's wife died. His second wife treated his two children cruelly and cursed Mr. Lu so much that he ran away. While running, he fell into a hole and found himself in a house with his deceased parents and his first wife. She does not want to recognize him. But Mr. Lu's father, hearing about the mistreatment of the children, orders her to return to earth as long as the children are small. On Mr. Lu's way back, she disappears. When Lu meets his children, they tell him that the stepmother at first continued to mistreat them, then lost consciousness, and after recovery behaved exactly like their dead mother. She now brings the household back into its former shape, and by showing her husband how his weakness toward his second wife—a sinful behavior—had brought on the intolerable conditions, she makes him feel ashamed. When the children are grown up and engaged, she leaves, and the second wife takes over the body which had been used by the first wife. The second wife had been forced to serve the in-laws in the netherworld and had been reformed by them (*Hsieh-to,* 7, 2a–3b).

---

[7] The texts are listed in historical order in each category.

[8] These two cases, (2) and (3), are not again treated in chapter vi. Other cases of suicide in this category of exposure are discussed in chapter vi.

(5) A poor woman and a woman from an educated family both lost their bridegrooms before the wedding had taken place. The father of the poor woman forces her to marry another man. The educated girl is forced by her family to remain a "chaste widow." When the poor woman visited the other one, the brother of the educated told her that she had lost her honor by remarrying. The poor, deeply offended, died and her soul went into the body of the chaste widow, who died at the same moment. The poor wife, in the body of the educated one, now has herself brought into the house of the educated bridegroom, lives there as "chaste widow" and acquires by this action so much prestige that her adopted son (a boy adopted by the parents of the dead groom to serve as his son and to continue the family line), who became a scholar, was allowed to erect an honorary monument to celebrate her chastity, an action which raised the prestige of the whole family. The woman now called the brother of the educated woman (who had not noticed that his sister had died and that her body was taken over by the soul of the other woman) and accused him of his bad behavior. He should have evaluated the motives and not the visible actions of the poor woman. By doing so, she makes him feel deeply ashamed (Hsieh-to, 9, 3a–4a). His sin was that he had caused the death of the poor woman.

(6) Parents wanted to dissolve the engagement of their daughter and refused to help her fiancé when he was poor. When they became poor and the fiancé was wealthy, they asked him for help. He refused help, reminding them of their past behavior, and thereby shamed them (Liao-chai, 6; V, 187–192). (7) A son discovered that his mother had a lover and murdered him. Rather than to tell the truth and thus to shame the mother, he preferred to be executed (Yüeh-wei ts'ao-t'ang pi-chi, 23, pp. 7–8). (8) A man told his sister-in-law that her disease was the punishment for her jealousy. When she denied having the disease, he proved it and shamed her (Liao-chai, XV, 5b–7a).

(9) A woman enticed several men who wanted to make love to her into a forest and made them hang their clothes on tree branches. The naked men are shamed (Yeh-t'an sui-lu, pp. 38–42). (10) A widow offered herself to a guest. When he refused her, she felt shamed and repented (Hsieh-to, 3, 8a–b). (11) A man saw a woman naked. She felt shamed (Erh-ju, 2, 1b–2a). (12) A desperately poor widow, in order to get the money for the burial of her husband, had herself undressed and beaten in public, substituting for some convicted woman who paid her for the substitution. She did not feel shamed, and her action was praised (Erh-ju, 2, 10a–b).

(13) A man murdered his bride when he noticed that she was already pregnant. Her family kept quiet in order to cover up her shame

(*Erh-ju*, 3, 12a). (14) A woman who had had sexual relations with animals is conducted publicly through the city to shame her (*Mai-yü-chi*, 2, 2a). (15) A courtesan who had pretended to be in love, rejected the man as soon as a wealthier one arrived. She was shamed when it was made public that the "wealthy" man was in reality a dressed-up beggar (*T'un-k'u lan-yen*, 104–105). (16) A scholar flirted with a girl. She shamed him by cutting off his beard (*T'un-k'u lan-yen*, 64–65).

Sinful Acts, Suspected to have been Committed, or Committed Without Knowledge or Intent—(1) A girl is raped; she feels shame (*Chin-ku ch'i-kuan*, Text 26). (2) A scholar is accused of having stolen a chicken. To prove his innocence he submits to the oracle of a deity. The oracle, too, seems to prove his guilt. He is publicly shamed, yet (as becomes known years later) innocent (*T'un-k'u lan-yen*, 148–149, and *Hsieh-to*, 6, 4b–5a). (3) A man came under the suspicion of entertaining sexual relations with a male orphan. He died of shame (*Yüeh-wei ts'ao-t'ang pi-chi*, 23, 6).

(4) When a scholar kidnapped a girl, her family kept quiet and pretended that she had married into a family far away from home, in order to hide the shame. When she is returned, her father refused to accept her back into the house (*Erh-ju*, 2, 12a–b). (5) A woman fought off a rapist. Yet she committed suicide later, feeling too much ashamed (*Mai-yü-chi*, 2, 1a–b). (6) A woman is murdered by a rapist. In spite of her chastity, the family felt so ashamed that no one was permitted to talk about the case (*Mai-yü-chi*, 2, 1a). (7) A landlord, stating that rent payments (in kind) were of bad quality, shamed the tenant in public. He and his family committed suicide (*Yung-wan pi-chi*, 4, 13a).

Exposure of Conceit, Ignorance, or Mistakes—(1) A Taoist did not recognize an imposter, and harm was caused. He felt shamed (*Kui-tung*, 1, 3b–4a). (2) A scholar flirted with a girl. She shamed him by showing that neither money nor titles impressed her (*Hsieh-to*, 9, 2b–3a). (3) A man boasted with his erudite manners. His host proved to him that he used empty forms, bare of true erudition, and shamed him by not letting him enter the house (*Hsieh-to*, 3, 7b). (4) A courtesan proved to a scholar that he was as worthless as she was. He felt shamed (*Hsieh-to*, 5, 6b–7a).

(5) A farmer asked a scholar to write a poem on his fan. He did this carelessly and made many mistakes. The farmer, in reality a scholar, corrected the mistakes and thus shamed him (*Hsieh-to*, 12, 2b). (6) A village girl proved to a scholar how ignorant he was and shamed him in this way (*Hsieh-to*, 9, 1a–b). (7) The ignorance of a so-called scholar is

publicly exposed (*Hsieh-to,* 7, 6b–7a). (8) A girl proved to a scholar how ignorant he was (*Hsieh-to,* 2, 5n–6a).

(9) A ghost shamed a scholar by publicly exposing his ignorance (*Hsieh-to,* 5, 7b–8a). (10) Merchants praised poems which were composed supposedly by a deity, but rejected poems made by a young scholar. He shamed them by announcing that both kinds of poems were composed by himself (*Hsieh-to,* 3, 2a–4a). (11) The ignorance of a scholar is exposed (*T'un-k'u lan-yen,* pp. 65–67).

CHAPTER SIX

Suicide in Short Stories

Categories

It may be remembered that in the *shan-shu* special attention was given to suicide. In certain cases with compelling reasons, suicide was regarded as morally justified; in other cases it was considered a sin. In order to clarify the relation of suicide to sin and guilt, all eighty-eight cases of suicide found in over sixteen hundred short stories were analyzed.[1] In other words, slightly over 5 percent of the stories contain suicides, and 78 percent of them were committed by women. Although there are no statistics on suicide for traditional China before 1900—and all our stories were written before 1900—one has the feeling that female suicides were indeed more common than male suicides in traditional China.[2] Our material gives the impression that suicides were more a topic of

[1] The collection consists this time of 1685 texts. All dramas and folktales have been excluded, but a number of other short-story texts, which I studied only recently and which were not included in chapter v, have been included here. With this type of material no selection of stories can ever claim to be "representative," and a "random" selection from the Chinese literature is an absurdity. Therefore, I analyzed simply all stories which I had read up to a certain time; but when I selected stories for reading I did not intend to collect data on suicides. Therefore, my selection is not biased with respect to this topic. The texts, not included in chapter v but used here, are mainly the *Hsieh-to* (122 stories) of the late eighteenth century, the *Erh-ju* of the nineteenth century, and a few single stories of earlier centuries.

[2] This seems not to be true in modern Taiwan. Taiwan, with a relatively high ratio of suicides (16.2 per 10,000 in 1960), had in 1960 six female suicides per ten male suicides, as many as that of Japan and more than in most Western countries. Suicide was committed mainly by poison (64.7 percent males, 55 percent females), but women often drowned themselves (13.7 percent males, 27.5 percent females). Reasons for suicides, according to police information, were mainly "household problems," followed by "economic troubles," "forced marriage," and "loss of beloved" (see Wu Hsi-chang, "A Comparative Study of the Problem of Suicide," *Shê-hui tao-chih,* Vol. 1 [1964], No. 2, pp. 21–28; Taipei, in Chinese).

literature in the seventeenth and nineteenth centuries than in other centuries, but this impression may be erroneous.

It goes without saying that the following is neither a sociological nor a psychological study of suicide. It is the manifest content of the stories, in so far as they reveal concepts of sin and guilt, that is of relevance here. Nevertheless, we tried out the well-known sociological categories of suicide,[3] but although I decided to use the names of two of them, the system as a whole does not fit the Chinese situation. Particularly the third category is not applicable: there are no anomic suicides reported; in fact, no writer in traditional China would have described any situation as an anomie. There are a few cases that one might label "samsonitic" suicide, namely suicide for the purpose of becoming a ghost and in that form to punish another person, or suicide in order to bring another person into serious difficulties. Such cases, especially of the second kind, are repeatedly told in Western writings about China, and one might feel tempted to classify some of the cases reported in the literature in this way. However, in each of these cases the suicide was involved with a violation of moral rules, a motif evidently more significant than spitefulness or even revenge. Also, the Chinese writers did not give explanations that would justify a category of samsonitic suicides. It was, therefore, attempted to classify suicides into categories which fit the Chinese material and which are directly or indirectly implied by the Chinese writers.

Under *altruistic suicides* I understand suicides committed in the interest of another person or an abstract concept. The sixteen cases in this category are overwhelmingly cases of loyalty either to the state or the dynasty, or to the husband. All sixteen of these suicides would be judged by the authors of the *shan-shu* as justified, honorable, and not sinful.

There were only twelve cases which might be classified as *egotistic suicide,* and this group is the only one in which a majority is male. In essence, these persons committed suicide either because they felt predestined by fate or because they could no longer endure life. According to tradition, these persons should have been aware that the present life is the result of acts in a former life and they should have accepted life. Therefore, the authors of the *shan-shu* would judge these suicides as not honorable but sinful. The short-story authors did not pass judgment but simply reported these cases. They neither praised nor excused the suicides.

The third class of suicides occurring in the stories are suicides committed because the person had *violated a moral rule.* Following the

[3] Emile Durkheim, *Suicide* (Glencoe, 1951); Ruth Cavan, *Suicide* (Chicago, 1928).

shan-shu rules, one can make some subclassifications. There is a group of suicides who *violated knowingly* a moral precept and paid the price for it by committing suicide. Such persons are sinners and the suicide is not an atonement but at best a self-inflicted punishment to which (the *shan-shu* would say) another punishment in the hells will certainly be added. All these suicides are not honorable because their cause is a sin. More interesting is a large group of suicides in which a *sin was committed without the intention* of doing it or even against the conscious will of the actor. Such situations are tragic in the classical sense. Chinese moralistic literature has taken the position that a sin is a sin, whether committed willingly and knowingly or not, just as a crime is punished as a crime, whatever the reason for the crime.[4] Our short-story writers were not as harsh as were the moralists. They report such cases with recognition and a certain approval as cases of courage or moral stamina. They certainly knew that only a few persons ever have the courage to expiate a sin committed unknowingly, or unwillingly—a sin for which the individual could not be expected to feel guilt. From our point of view, many of these cases are cases of shame. We could say, for instance, that a woman who was raped could not face the shame that society would heap upon her and, perhaps, the slanderous intimation that she had secretly wanted to commit adultery and had only pretended to be raped. In fact, this was probably the normal attitude of society in such a case. Yet, the moralists would not introduce the concept of shame to explain these suicides. The writers of short stories would do so only occasionally, and more easily in cases in which the act of sin was knowingly committed.

Between these two categories of suicide involving the violation of a moral rule is the next category: suicide as the result of a *dilemma*. The dilemma can be that there is a *conflict of moral rules* which the actor cannot solve satisfactorily. Whatever action is taken, it will lead to the breach of at least one precept; or one moral command can be fulfilled only by breaking another. We would, from our Western standpoint, regard all such cases as truly tragic, and we would appreciate the attempt to reconcile two conflicting rules, or to live up to *one* high command though this involved the breach of another. The Chinese writers seem to regard all these cases sympathetically, feeling much as we do. At least they acknowledge the courage and determination of the actors. The Chinese moralist is more likely to underline the guilt where sin is

---

[4] We might add here that sinful acts committed by persons who, according to our judgment, but also according to Chinese judgment, were mentally sick, are evaluated and punished just as if they had been committed by sane persons. In such cases, it could be argued that the sickness as such is a punishment for sins committed in a former life. Sins committed by sick persons only show that they deserve even further punishment.

involved, and to regard only such suicides as honorable in which no sinful act has occurred.

The last category—dilemma situations in which *no action* whatsoever seems *appropriate*—also presents difficulties to Chinese moralists. Most likely they would have regarded the reported solutions as extreme actions which should have been avoided.

It is interesting to see that our fairly large collection of short stories does not report simple love-suicides, which were fairly common among non-Chinese native tribes and in Japan as the result of an anomic situation, namely, clashes of different moral codes relative to marriage. Nor do we find a single case of egotistic suicide of Western type, such as the suicide of a lonely old person who had lost contact with society. Suicide by boys and girls during the period of puberty, so common in Western literature, are also completely missing. In fact I do not remember a single text describing unmistakably a desperate juvenile situation of this type, not even one not leading to suicide. One may read that a boy did not want to study and that this led to tensions between him and his father; or that he refused to marry when his parents wished him to. But no resulting suicides have been described, nor has the situation been taken as a serious one; rather, the Chinese writers explained such cases as temporary failures in character formation through education, and they were expected to be overcome eventually.

Needless to say, modern psychologists analyzing these cases of suicide would offer different explanations. It must be remembered that we were here interested only in the way in which the Chinese writers have explained suicides, and especially in the question whether it was shame or guilt that was most important in causing suicide. It appeared that even when an element of shame was directly or indirectly admitted, the stress was upon the aspects of sin and guilt in those suicides where the underlying behavior was sinful. But while sin was the cause, the suicide itself was not necessarily sinful but "justified" and was often, or even usually, looked upon as an admirable attempt to expiation, or the only way to avoid further sin. Secondly, there are the cases of "honorable" suicide which are not caused by sin on the part of the individual and are often committed precisely in order to avoid sin, or sin and shame. Thirdly, there are those tragic conflict situations beyond the individual's control. The Chinese writers seem to agree that the individual caught in such a situation is free of guilt (even though the same acts in a different context may be sinful and constitute guilt), and that this suicide is not sinful but justifiable and sometimes even honorable, since it appears to be the only or the most honorable solution. In other words, in China the tragic situation did not, as in Greece, produce a guilty hero. Finally, and in contrast, there are "unwarranted suicides" which are not caused by sins, but sometimes involve shame; these suicides are sinful in themselves and, as the reader already knows, are punished in hell.

Stories of Eighty-eight Cases of Suicide

HONORABLE (ALTRUISTIC) SUICIDE (ELEVEN WOMEN, FIVE MEN)

(1) When the Mongols deposed the dynasty, the imperial concubines wanted to remain loyal to the dynasty and their husband and committed suicide (*Shan-chü hsin-hua,* Text 117). The suicide is honorable. (2) A wife commits suicide when her husband was drowned (*Liao-chai,* II, 249–252). Loyalty to husband. Honorable suicide. (3) A wife attempted suicide when her husband dies (*Liao-chai,* 2; V, 19–23). Justified as sign of loyalty to husband. (4) A woman committed suicide out of loyalty to the dynasty (*Hsieh-to,* 4, 49b). Justified.

(5) A bride committed suicide when she heard that her fiancé had been killed in an accident (*T'un-k'u lan-yen,* pp. 36–37). Her loyalty to her future husband makes this suicide praiseworthy.

(6) When the enemy conquered the city, a girl committed suicide (*T'un-k'u lan-yen,* pp. 110–111). Her loyalty to the state makes this suicide justifiable. (7) A bride committed suicide when she heard that her innocent fiancé had been killed in jail (*T'un-k'u lan-yen,* pp. 115–116). Suicide because of loyalty; praiseworthy.

(8) Several women committed suicide when the dynasty fell (*Yung-wan pi-chi,* 6, 6b–7a). Loyalty. In all such cases, the women had to fear that the rebels would rape them. To be raped would have meant that they had (though against their will) been unfaithful toward their husbands, a break of another loyalty. (9) Case like No. 8 (*T'un-k'u lan-yen,* p. 91). (10) Case like No. 8 (*T'un-k'u lan-yen,* pp. 120–121).

(11) A girl committed suicide when her fiancé was murdered and a rebel wanted to marry her (*T'un-k'u lan-yen,* pp. 69–71). Main motive seems to be her loyalty to her fiancé; if she married the rebel she would also have violated the moral rule that a marriage should be initiated by the parents and not be forced upon the bride. (12) A man committed suicide in order to punish as a ghost a criminal official who had destroyed the tomb of his friend (*Shan-chü hsin-hua,* Text 12). Loyalty to friend.

(13) A boy had helped his half-brother secretly and protected him against the bad stepmother. When this boy was caught by a tiger, the

half-brother committed suicide (*Liao-chai,* 2; V, 31–35). The son violated the rule of filial piety toward his mother by helping the half-brother, but fulfilled the rule of brotherly love at the same time. The half-brother should not have brought him into the danger by accepting his help. He committed suicide out of loyalty to his brother.

(14) A man attempted suicide when the dynasty was abolished (*Mai-yü-chi,* 9, 2a–b). Loyalty. (15) A man attempted suicide when rebels caught him (*T'un-k'u lan-yen,* pp. 24–26). Primarily loyalty to the state, though it is likely that he also was afraid the rebels would kill him. Praiseworthy. (16) A man committed suicide together with his concubines when bandits conquered the city (*T'un-k'u lan-yen,* pp. 82–83). Loyalty, similar to last case.

SINFUL (EGOTISTIC) SUICIDE (EIGHT MEN, FOUR WOMEN)

(1) A maniac committed suicide after having slain his family. This was considered predestined (*Sou-shen-chi,* 2, 1a). (2) An impoverished official committed suicide in total despair (*Chien-teng hsien-hua,* Franke trans., pp. 354–355). (3) A man is humiliated because of his humble social origins. Finally, he committed suicide (*Wang-shih fu-ch'ou chi*). (4) A poor soldier in despair attempted suicide (*Yeh-t'an sui-lu,* pp. 49–51).

(5) A man committed suicide when accused of murder, without awaiting the trial (*Yeh-t'an sui-lu,* p. 138). (6) When a powerful man put another one into jail and took away his valuable collections, the victim committed suicide (*Liao-chai,* 3; IV, 374–377). (7) A rich wife reproached her poor husband of his poverty. He committed suicide (*Liao-chai,* 12; IV, 313–318). (8) A man is so mistreated by a lower official that he committed suicide (*Yeh-t'an sui-lu,* pp. 122–124).

(9) A woman had consented to become a wife. When her husband jokingly told her that she had become a concubine and not a wife, she committed suicide (*Liao-chai,* VI, 397–401). (10) A courtesan committed suicide when her mother did not permit her to marry her friend (*T'un-k'u lan-yen,* pp. 158–159). (11) A courtesan married but was mistreated by the main wife. She committed suicide because her life was much worse than before (*T'un-k'u lan-yen,* pp. 136–137). (12) In one family, in the course of seventy years, six persons, mainly women, committed suicide. This was fate (*Yung-wan pi-chi,* 6, 5b–6a).

SUICIDE BECAUSE OF VIOLATION OF MORAL RULES

Justified Suicide to Expiate Guilt and Avoid Shame (eleven Women, four Men)—(1) A girl had sexual relations with a man. She committed suicide when he dropped her (*Chin-ku ch'i-kuan,* Text 35b). (2) A wife committed suicide when it was proved in public that she had been adulterous (*Chin-ku ch'i-kuan,* Text 20). Here, the element of shame is included, but adultery was already a sin which the woman intended to expiate by suicide. (3) A wife tried to separate her husband from his brothers. When her plans became known, she committed suicide (*Chin-ku ch'i-kuan,* Text 19). Here, too, the element of shame comes in, but to separate brothers is a sin.

(4) A husband disappeared. His wife, who had despised him, married another, rich man. When her husband returned, she committed suicide (*Liao-chai,* 12; IV, 313–318). The element of shame is important, but to be disloyal to the husband is a grave sin. (5) A girl had sexual relations with her fiancé. She committed suicide when he married another girl (*Hsieh-to,* 6, 3b–4a). Premarital sexual relations, even with the fiancé, are a grave sin. (6) An unmarried girl who became pregnant, committed suicide (*Liao-chai,* 4; II, 72–76). (7) An adulterous wife committed suicide (*T'un-k'un lan-yen,* pp. 78–79).

(8) A bride gives her fiancé money so that he could pay her bridal price. When he did not and disappeared, she committed suicide (*T'un-k'u lan-yen,* pp. 59–61). Personal relations of this kind between persons who are not married are sinful. (9) A girl committed suicide when her parents forbade her to marry her lover (*T'un-k'u lan-yen,* pp. 125–126). A girl should not have personal relations with a man before marriage. (10) Case like No. 8 (*T'un-ku' lan-yen,* pp. 84–85).

(11) A girl committed suicide when her lover repudiated her (*T'un-k'u lan-yen,* pp. 156–158). She had sinned by having relations before marriage. (12) When a rich man had become poor, monks fed him the rice he had carelessly thrown away when he was rich. He committed suicide when he found this out (*Chin-ku ch'i-kuan,* Text 22a). Throwing away food, especially rice, is a sin. The element of shame, of course, also enters here.

(13) A man had once seduced a girl. During his examination, he committed suicide (*Yeh-t'an sui-lu,* p. 98). We can assume that the ghost of the girl appeared and thus induced him to suicide. This was her revenge. (14) A servant had been accused of theft and had been executed. His master, who had committed the theft, committed suicide (*Yeh-t'an sui-lu,* pp. 103–104). Explanation probably like that in No. 13. (15) By a criminal monk, a gambler is brought into a situation in which he is forced to commit suicide (*Liao-chai,* XI, 33a–b). Gambling as such is a sin.

Justifiable Suicide when Sin was Committed without Will or Intention (Tragic) (fourteen Women, one Man)—(1) A servant girl, who had sexual relations with her master, committed suicide because of her illicit love (*Chien-teng hsien-hua,* Franke trans., p. 377). Sexual relations out of wedlock are a sin. But she could not prevent it because of her social position. (2) A mother let her daughter have sexual relations with a man who, she thought, was her fiancé. When she found out that he was an imposter, the girl committed suicide (*Chin-ku ch'i-kuan,* Text 24b). The mother should never have allowed her daughter to have premarital relations. But this would have been a minor sin. To let the daughter have premarital sexual relations with a stranger, ruined the whole life and marriage of the girl.

(3) A courtesan persuaded her lover, a rebel, to surrender to the government, which had promised to grant him amnesty. But, breaking this promise, they killed him. She committed suicide (*Wang T'sui-ch'iao chuan*). Although the girl had led a sinful life, she had attempted to do an act of loyalty to the government and at the same time to correct her lover's sinful life. Against her intentions, she caused his death. (4) When a man tried to kidnap a married wife, she attempted suicide (*Liao-chai,* 15; VI, 504–506). For a married woman, any contact with another man, even if this is forced upon her, is a sin.

(5) A married woman is kidnapped. She murdered the kidnapper, then committed suicide (*Liao-chai,* 6; VI, 521–525). Explanation as in No. 4. (6) A married wife took, without knowing, love drugs. As a consequence, she tried to seduce a house guest. She attempted suicide when she became aware of her act (*Liao-chai,* 14, 21a–b). Explanation as in No. 4. (7) A girl is kidnapped. She committed suicide (*Liao-chai,* 12; II, 239–242). Premarital relations, even if involuntary, are sinful. (8) A kidnapped wife committed suicide (*Liao-chai,* 3; I, 131–134). Explanation as in No. 4.

(9) A girl attempted suicide when kidnapped and sold as prostitute (*T'un-k'u lan-yen,* pp. 172–174). Explanation as in No. 7. (10) A married woman successfully fought off a raper. Yet, she committed suicide (*Mai-yü-chi,* 2, 1a–b). Explanation as in No. 4, but the element of shame entered into the case additionally. (11) A girl who had been kidnapped and forced to marry the kidnapper, who had the appropriate social status, committed suicide (*T'un-k'u lan-yen,* pp. 62–63). The man would have been a suitable husband, but premarital relations are sinful. (12) A girl was engaged to a man, but these plans came to nothing because of the greed of her father. She committed suicide (*Yung-wan pi-chi,* 6, 1a–2a). Not through her fault, she broke a promise.

(13) A married woman committed suicide after having been raped (*Mai-yü-chi,* 2, 1b–2a). (14) A man raped a girl, then exploited her financially, then left her. She committed suicide (*Erh-ju,* 1, 12b). (15)

A boy unintentionally killed an animal which his father had been ordered to catch and to bring to the court. He attempted suicide (*Liao-chai,* 7; V, 235–238). His act could have resulted in the execution of his father. It was an act of unfilial behavior.

Honorable Suicide in Dilemma Situations with Conflict of Norms (eighteen Women, one Man)—(1) A courtesan, wanting to remain faithful to her lover, committed suicide when an officer wanted to take her by force (*Chien-teng hsien-hua,* Franke trans., p. 369). As a courtesan, she had lost her honor and lived in sin. She wanted, however, to live up to the moral standards of a wife. Thus, she rejected another man, though by profession she should have accepted him. (2) A courtesan committed suicide when her lover dropped her (*Chin-ku ch'i-kuan,* Text 35a). Explanation similar to No. 1.

(3) A courtesan had given her lover money so that he could buy and marry her. When he planned to sell her again, she committed suicide (*Chin-ku ch'i-kuan,* Text 51). She had broken several moral rules, but by breaking the last one (giving money to a man) she had hoped to be able to become a true wife. When she realized that her husband still regarded her as a prostitute, she committed suicide. (4) The brother-in-law wanted to give his sister-in-law to another man in marriage during the absence of her husband. She committed suicide (*Chin-ku ch'i-kuan,* Text 31b). She was in a dilemma: as a wife she was not supposed to break the marriage; as a sister-in-law she was forced morally to obey her husband's brother.

(5) The father hated his daughter's husband and tried to create a situation in which he would die. She committed suicide (*Chin-ku ch'i-kuan,* Text 14). Morally, she was obliged to be filial to her father and to obey him. Yet, she also was obliged to remain faithful to her husband. (6) A girl had been raped. She committed all kinds of sinful acts, accepting shameful situations in order to be able to take revenge. After the revenge, she committed suicide (*Chin-ku ch'i-kuan,* Text 26). Her revenge was justified, but as the means for revenge had to be sinful, she could not live on after the revenge.

(7) A mother sold her daughter in order to pay the debts of her husband. When the money was stolen, she committed suicide (*Liao-chai,* VI, 420–424). To save the honor of her husband, a morally good act, she had to commit a sinful act, to sell the daughter. When, not through her fault, the good act could not be performed, she committed suicide. (8) A wife sold a concubine. The concubine attempted suicide (*Liao-chai,* V, 45–48). The concubine was on the one hand obliged to remain faithful to her husband; on the other hand obliged to obey the main wife.

(9) A courtesan reproached her lover as being corrupt. He mistreated her. She committed suicide (*Liao-chai*, II, 96–100). Fight against corruption is an act of loyalty. But as a courtesan, she had no right to give moral advice to a man. (10) A wife lost ornaments which she had borrowed. She was unable to repay them. The finder promised to return the ornaments if she permitted him to have sexual relations with her. She consented. In order to keep the wife, he murdered her husband. She committed suicide (*Liao-chai*, 16, 13a–14a). In order to fulfill one moral obligation (to return borrowed goods) she willingly violated another moral obligation (committed adultery) and unwillingly caused a supreme sin (the murder of her husband).

(11) The wife of a poor man consented to have herself sold to another man in order to have money to support her mother-in-law. When the lady died, she committed suicide (*Yüeh-wei ts'ao-t'ang pi-chi*, 23, 11). In order to fulfill one moral obligation, filial piety, toward the mother of her husband, she had consented to break another rule (faithfulness toward her husband).

(12) A girl had promised her poor fiancé some good food. Her parents found out about her attempt and blamed her strongly. She committed suicide (*Erh-ju*, 2, 14a). Premarital relations are sinful, even with the fiancé. But she had made a promise out of pity to the man and wanted to keep the promise.

(13) A bride committed suicide when she became aware that her mother had wanted the marriage only in order to remain able to continue illicit sex relations with that man (*Erh-ju*, 1, 13a). As a daughter, she was expected to obey her mother; but if she did so, she condoned a capital sin. (14) A wife exposed her husband's crime in order to save an innocent other man (*Mai-yü-chi*, 3, 4a–b). She was obliged to remain loyal to her husband, yet would have caused the death of an innocent man if she had remained loyal.

(15) A girl murdered a bandit and then committed suicide (*T'un-k'u lan-yen*, 22–23). To kill a bandit is a good act, an act of loyalty toward the state; but to have personal contacts with a man without being married to him is sinful. (16) A girl married the first man who was willing to pay for the burial of her mother. After this was done, she committed suicide (*T'un-k'u lan-yen*, 100–101). To provide a decent burial for the parents is an extremely good act. But to marry on one's own initiative, that is, to sell oneself to a man, is a sin.

(17) A man who was under obligation toward another man committed two murders for his benefactor. Then he committed suicide (*Liao-chai*, 6; V, 203). He had to be grateful to his benefactor, but a murder is a grave sin. (18) When her father had been murdered, the daughter accepted various humiliations, even became a whore (as such: sinful

behavior), in order to be able to take revenge. When revenge had been achieved, she committed suicide (*Liao-chai*, VI, 473–475). She apparently had no other way to fulfill a supreme duty: to take revenge for her father. Her sin was, therefore, understandable, but her suicide necessary.

(19) After her husband was murdered, the widow married the murderer, because only thus she could have her husband buried in a decent way. The murderer had promised to bury the victim in full splendor. She then had sexual relations with another man after that man had promised to murder her present husband, the murderer. After she had succeeded in revenging her first husband, she committed suicide (*Hsieh-to*, 4, 15a–16a). She had to commit suicide because she violated several of the most important moral rules. But her suicide is justifiable because only by this means she was able to fulfill two supreme duties: to bury her husband and to take revenge for her husband.

Justified Suicide in Dilemma Situations: The Actor Cannot Prove His Innocence, or Has no Other Way Out, or No Other Way to Avoid Sin or Shame (eleven Women)—(1) A man asserts that he had sexual relations with a married woman and supplies false proofs. As she could not prove her innocence, she committed suicide (*Liao-chai*, IV, 33a–b). (2) A girl is hairy. Her disgusted husband refused sexual relations. She attempted suicide (*Hsieh-to*, 10, 6b–7a). She had been married to the man according to the moral rules, and he had, therefore, the moral duty to have sexual relations with her. (3) A girl in extreme poverty is constantly besieged by a man who wants illicit sexual relations. She attempted suicide (*Liao-chai*, I, 199–205).

(4) A husband attempts to divorce his wife in order to be able to make his concubine his wife. The wife commits suicide (*Yung-wan pi-chi*, 6, 10b). She had no way to prevent her husband from committing an illegal act which would have brought her into disgrace (shame). (5) A wife committed suicide when her husband neglected the whole family completely (*Yung-wan pi-chi*, 6, 13a–b). She had no way to make him fulfill his moral obligations, yet she was morally not allowed to desert him. (6) A wife is under suspicion of having committed adultery and is unable to prove her innocence. She committed suicide (*Yung-wan pi-chi*, 4, 14b–15a). (7) A girl attempted suicide when her nurse attempted to sell her as a prostitute (*T'un-k'u lan-yen*, pp. 3–5). She had certain obligations toward the nurse, but not such obligations that would have forced her to commit a grave sin.

(8) A gambling husband lost his wife. She committed suicide (*T'un-k'u lan-yen*, pp. 59–60). She could not prevent him from committing the sin of gambling, but by accepting another man, she would

have committed a grave sin. (9) A girl committed suicide when her fiancé broke the engagement and married another girl (*Mai-yü-chi*, 2, 10a–11b). The break of the engagement would have meant that she was not faithful to the fiancé. But she could not prevent his act. (10) An official had promised to give a poor old woman her legal right. When he broke his promise, she committed suicide (*Yung-wan pi-chi*, 5, 5b–6a). (11) A whole family of seven committed suicide, when the landlord unjustifiedly cursed the tenant and shamed him in public (*Yung-wan pi-chi*, 4, 13a).

CHAPTER SEVEN

Moralists Evaluate Sin and Shame:
The T'ai-shang pao-fa t'u-shuo

We mentioned early in chapter II the *T'ai-shang pao-fa t'u-shuo* as an example of a *shan-shu,* a moralistic text for indoctrination of common people. On the other hand, the kinds of story this book contains are in their structure very similar to normal short stories written for the elite, with the difference that this book selects stories with a moral ending. It is interesting to compare these stories with those short stories which we analyzed above, stories which also had a moral ending but were written for the educated.

The Text

The book contains 206 stories in its main section, and all these stories deal with good and bad actions which are rewarded or punished. Our print is from 1903,[1] and although the editor, Huang Cheng-yüan, stated that he had it printed in 1755, a number of additions were made by later editors; the last of these is Mao Chin-lan in 1868–1869. Therefore, some of the supplementary stories play in the nineteenth century up to 1865 and 1869,[2] and the illustrations show rifles and bayonets.[3] I left aside these late additions, so that in the main the material used here represents mid-eighteenth century ideas.[4] The book relies on older books of the same type, especially on the *T'ai-shang kan-ying-p'ien,* which was translated into French in 1835, while the Chinese text was published by Fr. Turrettini in 1889.[5] Our text has numerous stories contained also in the

---

[1] I wish to express my thanks to Prof. Paul Serruys, who made a copy of this book available to me.

[2] Chapter 7, p. 48b.

[3] 6, 5a.

[4] The last story of the book, about Huang himself, mentions an event of 1765. The impression is given that he wrote this entry himself.

[5] Stanislas Julien, *Livres des récompenses et des peines* (Paris, 1835); François Turrettini, *Le livre des récompenses et des peines* (Texte Chinois, Génève, 1889).

Kan-ying-p'ien; however, it is more extensive and often the stories are greatly changed. Other stories are adapted from the classical literature, historical texts, novels, and even dramas.

In these cases the story is also often modified, in order to emphasize the moral. Of the 206 stories, 77 play at a definitely stated date in history (referred to as "dated stories" in the following paragraphs). Many of the remaining 129 stories, often with obviously fictitious names—like many dramas—do not indicate the exact time when the events were supposed to have taken place (referred to as "undated stories"). All stories are reported as if they were true stories, although some are clearly and provably not historical. There are some notable differences between the dated and the undated stories: the heroes in the dated stories are much more often members of the upper class than those in the other stories (77.9 percent versus 35.7 percent).[6] The authors of these stories probably assumed that the reader would be more impressed if the persons punished for their sins were persons of the upper class. On the other hand, the dated stories mention sexual affairs less often than the undated stories (16.8 percent versus 22 percent). The dated stories show a distribution which one might expect: there are no stories about events earlier than the Han time (206 B.C.), and the closer to the present time, the more stories; there are, however, particularly many stories playing in the Ming period. Not all stories report only sins, but some contain also good actions; but the dated stories report slightly more sinful than praiseworthy actions.

If we compare, among the dated stories, those playing early in history with those playing in more recent times, there are no great differences. Some stories of rare sins were located in the remote past. Probably it was not easy to find a "true" story of a man who spit when a meteorite fell—a fairly serious sin, for which a case from the third century was selected.[7] Other rare cases were: devilish cults involving human sacrifices;[8] secretly feeding monks with food they were not allowed to eat;[9] serving different rulers simultaneously (at a period when China had two dynasties at the same time);[10] sorcery changing men into donkeys;[11] or killing trees belonging to others by the use of poison.[12] The more recent stories seem to mention sex more often and certainly are more concerned with the problem of loyalty.

[6] Only in 6.5 percent is the class origin unclear; in 21 percent of the undated is the class not given.

[7] 8, 14a-b.

[8] 7, 2a-b; a case of Han time.

[9] 6, 64a-b; happened around 500 A.D.

[10] 6, 44a-b; happened around 500 A.D.

[11] 5, 59a-b; a case of T'ang time.

[12] 5, 62a-b; a case of T'ang time.

The undated stories, many of which probably are of recent origin—in fact, the author indicated this in his preface—obviously were not selected by the editor on the basis of local reports around his home (Lo-yüan in Fukien province); most of the stories indicating the place of action located the scene in the Yangtze River area (Central China; 60 percent of all localized undated stories, but only 40 percent of all localized dated stories), while fewer undated stories played in the North (30 percent undated, but 53 percent dated). Studies of the regions occurring frequently in stories indicate that (a) the more recent the supposed time of the stories, the more often they are localized in Central China; the earlier, the more in the North; and (b) the more middle-class persons are heroes of stories, the more often they take place in Central China. Both statements are true also of our book (undated stories have over 30 percent middle-class heroes, dated, only 9 percent).

Shame in the T'ai shang pao-fa t'u-shuo

We should hardly expect a treatment of shame in a book which deals specifically with sin. Yet, our text mentions relatively more cases of shame than do other short stories (8.2 percent of all stories against 2 percent in other short stories). However, all cases except one can be regarded as cases where sinful acts believed to be unknown, or at least unknown to the public, are made public.

In the one case which seems to belong in the category of suspected sinful acts, the author is interested in the consequences of slander, which is a sin; he is not at all interested in an evaluation of the aspect of shame. The total absence of shame cases dealing with ignorance and conceit is no surprise: as was mentioned, such cases do not involve sin and, therefore, the author of this book on sin did not include such cases.

Let me summarize the seventeen cases involving shame which I found in the *T'ai-shang pao-fa t'u-shuo*:

(1) A man slanders another one and even attempts to murder him. The slandered man does not take revenge when the slanderer later comes into trouble. The slanderer feels very much ashamed (4, 6a). Slander is a sin. (2) A man insults his teacher, saying that he has never achieved anything in life. When the teacher attains a high position, he returns the slanderous remark. The pupil feels ashamed (3, 30a–b). A pupil has to honor his teacher; to slander him is a sin. (3) A man steals the examination papers of a friend and is appointed to high offices. When the friend much later reaches higher offices, the thief is so ashamed that he resigns from his job (2, 53a). Theft is a sin.

(4) A poor scholar is the victim of derision by his brothers-in-law. When he has reached high position, he takes revenge and shames the brothers-in-law publicly (7, 60a–b). Derision is a sin. (5) A man's brother's wife, wishing for her children to inherit their uncle's property, curses his childless wife. She acquires concubines for her husband, so that he becomes the father of five children. Thereupon the childless wife shames her hostile sister-in-law publicly (5, 42a–b). To cause hostility in the family is a sin.

(6) Wife and children of an arrogant man were put out naked on the street by bandits as a revenge (5, 4a–b). Although banditry is sinful, to be arrogant is sinful, too. (7) When a man got poor, his former bondsman accused him of moral faults. When the poor man later returned to high honors, he shamed the subordinate in public (5, 53a–b). As a subordinate he could have attempted to guide his master, but never more. To accuse him wrongly is a grave sin.

(8) A man sells his wife against her will to another man. Much later, when the husband is in prison, accused of theft and completely degenerated, she pays for him so that he is freed, thus shaming him severely (7, 26a–b). To sell a wife is a very serious sin. (9) When a wife committed adultery, her husband felt so ashamed that he did not go to court (6, 40a–b). (10) A man serves six lords, which is a shameful lack of loyalty (5, 6a). Disloyalty is a sin.

(11) An ugly man is constantly ridiculed. When he received a position higher than the other man, he sent him a poem which shamed him (5, 55a). Derision is a sin. (12) A man stole a book on strategy and had success in war until in the presence of the emperor his deed became known. He is deeply ashamed (4, 45a–b). (13) Through dishonesty a man reached the highest posts. When he tried to read to the emperor a poem made by another man, his cheating became public. He was ashamed (5, 12a–b).

(14) A nephew who is sure he will inherit his childless uncle's property derides the uncle. But the uncle got a son and shamed the nephew in public (5, 51a–b). A case much like No. 5. (15) A rich man humiliated a scholar whom he did not recognize as an educated man. He even attempted to take his wife from him. The scholar later induced the rich man to treat him again like a beggar. Then he invited the rich man into his house and shamed him by forcing him to eat on the floor like an animal (5, 51a–b). A case like No. 4.

(16) A man cancels the engagement of his daughter with a poor man in order to find a richer husband for her. When the repudiated man received a high post, he shamed the man (4, 10a–b). To break an engagement is a sin. (17) Bandits rob a woman, undress her, and tie her

up. A relative slanders her by saying she had been raped. Her husband is so much ashamed that he leaves her (4, 51a–b). This case belongs in the category "Sinful facts suspected to have been committed."

One trait which occurs only occasionally in short stories appears rather frequently in this book: people get into shameful situations after mistreating poor persons, not realizing that high and low status, wealth and poverty may change. I know of no nonreligious text which stresses the impermanence of social status as much as this one. Yet, it should be remarked that the *T'ai-shang pao-fa t'u-shuo* does not really stress social mobility. Changes are temporary, the result of good, moral actions. The Introduction mentions that persons who study the book may have success in business or in their official career, long life, many sons, few sicknesses, no political trouble, no separation of father and son, and in the most fortunate case it might happen that the whole family would ascend to heaven—though this once took four generations of incessant ardor.[13] In general, this book and all *shan-shu,* as well as practically all short stories and dramas, conceive of a well-ordered social world where everybody has his place. Only temporary upward mobility can occur, as a result of good deeds, while downward mobility is more common and more permanent, as a consequence of sin.

Suicide

It is understandable that the *Pao-fa t'u-shuo* discusses a greater number of reports on suicide than do other short stories (11 percent of all stories in the book). And while the percentage of women committing suicide is similar in both sources (almost 70 percent in the *Pao-fa,* 78 percent in the short stories), the kinds of suicide differ in their frequency. Let me first discuss the twenty-three cases.

ALTRUISTIC SUICIDE

(1) (2) (3) Suicide of a man at the end of the dynasty (3, 22a–b); loyalty to the ruler. (4) A military leader committed suicide when his plans led to a military disaster (3, 22a–b). This case is not clear: the book criticized the man because of the basic cruelty of his plans. Moreover, if he had not committed suicide, he most likely would have been executed. Yet, we could also regard the case as altruistic, as a sacrifice in the service of his country. (5) A girl committed suicide in order to help prove the innocence of an accused (4, 18a).

[13] Introduction, pp. 4b–14a.

EGOTISTIC SUICIDE

(6) A man who was deeply in debt and whose wife was about to give birth to another child, committed suicide in despair (2, 45a–b). (7) After a series of blows of fortune, a man committed suicide (2, 2a–b). (8) A concubine was so mistreated by the main wife that she committed suicide (4, 60a–b). (9) A live-in son-in-law was so mistreated that he planned suicide (7, 32a–33a).

DILEMMA CASES

Suicide to Expiate Guilt—(10) A man, pursued by a revengeful ghost, committed suicide (2, 3a–b). (11) Neighbors threaten an adulteress of whose actions they disapprove; she commits suicide (4, 12a). (12) A man repudiated his main wife and married another one. The ghost of the repudiated wife induced husband and second wife to commit suicide (5, 2a–b).

Sin Committed Against Intentions—(13) A courtesan persuaded her lover, a rebel, to surrender after amnesty had been promised. He was treacherously killed. She committed suicide (4, 4a–b). This case is the same which is discussed in chapter VI, on suicide in short stories. The case, incidentally, is also immortalized in dramas. (14) A seduced nun committed suicide (1, 22a–b). (15) A woman kidnapped by bandits committed suicide (4, 47a–b). (16) A woman is taken by force away from her husband by a powerful man. She committed suicide (4, 58a–b). (17) A widow understood that her second husband did not marry her out of commiseration for her situation, but had murdered the husband in order to get her. She committed suicide. (5, 44a–45a). Her re-marriage was a regrettable act, forgivable only because of her poverty. But by accepting the man's marriage offer, she indirectly had murdered her husband.

Conflict of Norms—(18) A girl's engagement was broken because of loose talk of her brother. She was married to another man, whereupon she committed suicide (5, 2a–b). On the one hand, she had the obligation to keep the engagement, because a break of an engagement is similar to a loss of chastity. On the other hand, she had to obey her family, even if her brother acted irresponsibly. (19) A wife committed suicide and thus covered up the crimes of her husband (7, 20a–b). She should not hide crimes, but she also should not let her husband die.

No Way to Prove Innocence—(20) Two servant girls committed suicide because they had been accused of theft and could not prove their innocence (5, 20a–b). (21) A wife became pregnant during the absence of her husband. Swearing her innocence, she promised to commit suicide if the delivery did not prove her case. She gave birth to a monster; thus her innocence is proved (8, 10a–b). (22) A bride committed suicide when she was accused in court of being pregnant. She was not (3, 24a–b). (23) A wife was accused of having sexual relations with a monk. Although this was not the case, she committed suicide (3, 32a).

The *Pao-fa* appears to be less interested in cases of conflict of norms. It contains only two cases, and the main interest is not the tragic conflict but the man's sin which brought the woman into the situation of conflict and suicide. For a moralistic book it is logical to identify moral rules and sinful transgressions, and to avoid cases in which it is difficult or impossible to decide which rule should be followed. Similarly, in all cases of dilemma the *Pao-fa* only aims at showing the consequences of sin for the sinner, so that the focus is often not on the person who committed suicide. By contrast, in the short stories the complex problem of dilemma appears to be much more important than the exposure of sin. The simple moralistic preaching of the *Pao-fa* is certainly the reason that its stories are so much less interesting, even if they were taken from short-story sources; their simplemindedness made scholars and educated persons deride this kind of literature, much to the scorn of *shan-shu* writers.

Special Features of Some of the Stories

The *Pao-fa* follows older books (especially the *Kan-ying-ching*) by going systematically through the different categories of sin, giving an example for each sin. In its evaluation of sins it does not deviate from the other books, but some of the stories illustrate some attitudes more clearly than do the more theoretical texts. One important aspect of the *Pao-fa,* which it shares with other books of this kind, is its orthodox position on questions of Confucianism. The *Pao-fa* depicts men like Wang An-shih,[14] Ts'ai Ching,[15] and Li Cho-wu,[16] who during their lifetime had expressed unorthodox views, as criminals of the worst kind without any attempt to evaluate their actions. Men of the T'ang time, like

[14] 3, 56a-b; he was reborn as a pig.
[15] 3, 28a; he was executed.
[16] 4, 25a-b; he was executed.

Li Pi,[17] or of the Sung, like Szu-ma Kuang [18] and Han Ch'i,[19] who are models of Confucian behavior, are praised without restraint. Men who criticized Confucianism, like Meng-tzu, are seen suffering in hell for this crime,[20] although persons who hate moralistic religious books of Buddhist type are also severely punished.[21] On the other hand, persons who write novels [22] suffer for such frivolity by being executed, or by long tortures in hell.[23] But the *Pao-fa* mentions famous Chinese military heroes only rarely and does not praise them too highly, although it lauds loyalty to the ruler. In this attitude, the *Pao-fa* deviates strongly from the traditional drama which extols the actions of military leaders. Foreigners, expecially Indian Buddhists, are not mentioned at all, in spite of the role they played in religious writings.

Ghost stories are also rare in the *Pao-fa* and no fox story is given. Some of the short-story collections have a special love for this kind of story because it gives the author an excuse to discuss erotic matters. The *Pao-fa* has a number of cases of obsession by ghosts, but only to give the ghost an opportunity to tell, through the mouth of a sinner, what sins the obsessed had committed. Such obsession is normally of short duration and the ghost is not related to the obsessed. As a rule, exorcism is not necessary, but sacrifices have to be performed after the ghost has gone. A ghost who is not a former family member has to be exorcised if he does not leave quickly on his own, while ghosts who had been family members during their life, have to be honored by sacrifices while they speak through the mouth of the victim but need not be exorcised. It would be interesting to analyze the social function of these two types of mental disease (if we are allowed to use modern terminology), but the *Pao-fa* does not have enough data for such a study. The book has still two other forms of mental disease which are both explained as results of sin. In one case the disease is explained as a punishment meted out by a offended deity:

Mr. Fei made fun of the god of the hearth and the ceremonies feasting him. Afterwards, a fight broke out between Mr. Fei's wife and his beloved servant girl, in which Fei took the girl's side. The wife cried in front of the altar of the deity. During the night, Mr. Fei was found in front of the altar,

[17] 2, 61a-b.
[18] 3, 8a.
[19] 2, 49a.
[20] 4, 23a–b.
[21] 7, 50a-b; he hated the story of Mu-lien, who entered hell in order to save his mother from deserved punishments.
[22] Like Juan Ta-ch'eng, seventeenth century.
[23] 7, 42a-b; authors of erotic stories mentioned.

beating his head on the floor until it was bloody. He was out of his mind. After he was feeling better, he said that two spirits had picked him up, forced him to kneel down, had cursed him and given him a drink. Since then, he could not remember a single letter and, thus, could no longer compose satirical poems. He also was unable to feel hunger and sexual desire (8, 4a-b).

Fei had committed two sins: he had offended the god and his wife in front of the altar. His mental sickness is explained as a consequence of sin. In another case, the situation was more complex:

When a woman sacrificed in a temple, the judge-deity smiled and visited her at night, expressing the wish for sexual relations. Refusing, she ran away, finally flew and landed on top of a pagoda. When she went down, she came into a bedroom where she met the judge. Now she could not refuse him and lived with him. During the day, he went out and did his job of meting out punishment to sinners; at night he returned with food for her. In a conversation with him she learned that a person can improve his fate by reciting the Kuan-yin sutra. This she did, with the result that the judge-deity became unable to have sexual relations with her. She was miraculously returned to her own house and bed. It was found out that only her soul, not her body, had had sexual relations with the deity (2, 14a-b).

The author wanted to exemplify the beneficial consequences of reading Buddhist texts, as well as the deplorable fact that deities can commit immoral acts. Modern psychiatry would regard this case as one of delusion. The text gives an ingenious twist to the story so that the woman comes out innocent without having committed a sin. Only actual intercourse would have counted against her. Thus, the woman remains a member of society and does not have to commit suicide.

The *Pao-fa* agrees with the books on sin that animals cannot commit sins because they are not themselves responsible. The following story illustrates this by showing that the tiger could kill only after it had been given permission:

A repenting bandit who slept in a temple of a mountain god heard a tiger entering. The tiger prayed to the god for food. The god granted him a pig which would wash laundry at the river the next morning. When the bandit went to the river in the morning and saw that the "pig" was a girl, he saved her and killed the tiger. Then he accused the god of immorality and smashed his figure. Doing this he "changed," that is, he died. Later he appeared to the farmers and explained that he had been nominated as successor to the god. He was so moralistic that he did not want to inherit the widow of the former god, so her statue had to be moved into another room of the temple (8, 34a–b).[24]

---

[24] Another version of this story without, however, the detail about the god's wife, is in *Hsiang-yin-lou pin-t'an*, I, 17b–18a, written before 1880.

On the other hand, as in the books on sin, sinners are often punished by infliction of punishment or death on their family members. We find no consideration for the suffering of the innocent, as in the following two stories:

Mr. Ch'i thought he was a good Confucian by being against the folk religion. Thus, while living in a temple, he used a statue of a deity as firewood, when all other wood was wet. In a dream, a deity told him that fate had destined him to a high position in life, but that because of these deeds, half of his lifetime had been taken away from him. When he woke up, he still was not afraid. On the contrary, he stated that the deities probably were afraid of him, because they had not beaten him. Thus, he secretely burned the statues to which his mother used to pray. Much later, after the age of forty, he failed in all examinations, became a drinker, whored, and at the same time had homosexual relations. But his men friends seduced his wife. Some days later he was brought into hell where he was punished to stay in the deepest hell for eons. He woke up once more, told about his future and died. Both his sons were cripples and his family died out (1, 24a–b).

Mr. Chu got a son from his wife and at the same time a son from his concubine. The son of the concubine was extremely industrious and frugal; the other one was a wastrel. One day, the concubine's son got sick and said: "Now I have, through my work, repaid my debt to you" and died. Soon, the other one also died, saying that he had wasted as much money as Mr. Chu had owed him in a former life. Chu found this unfair and complained. His son advised him to do meritorious deeds. As a consequence, Mr. Chu had two more sons (6, 52a–b).

In both cases, sons, and in the first story also the wife, have to suffer for sins which they did not commit. This unfair treatment does not bother our author at all. He focuses only on the sinner and the effect his actions have upon him.

As we have said, according to the books on sin, sinful actions even if committed unknowingly [25] are punished; and actions by persons who in our opinion are mentally sick and therefore not responsible are also explained as actions for which the consequences have to be borne. This religion, then, has a "legalistic" attitude: a case is a case, whatever are the reasons for it. In contrast, Confucianism shows a much more psychological attitude by weighing each individual case. It has been pointed out that legalist philosophy is egalitarian and that the legalists were amoral and pragmatic; [26] they believed in law and wanted to apply the law uniformly without taking the person into account, because of their belief that man is basically bad, moved only by self-interest. It took a long time

[25] A very pious person killed a man by giving him a medicine which he thought would help him. All his piety did not outweigh the "murder" (2, 8a-b).

[26] Charles Hucker, "Confucianism and the Chinese Censorial System," in Arthur Wright, *Confucianism and Chinese Civilization* (New York, 1964), p. 65.

until Chinese criminal law, which is built on Legalist theories, took insanity into account,[27] although already from 120 A.D. on, insane persons received lighter punishments than normal persons.[28]

The *Pao-fa* finds itself—as do other texts of this kind—in a difficult situation when fate is discussed. It believes in fate: the conditions of life are determined from birth because they are a consequence of actions in the former life. But it also finds it necessary to accept a measure of flexibility:

Mr. Chao, apparently a gentleman, always had secret plans. One day, he induced a servant in hell, whom he knew personally, to look up in the book his own fate. He learned that he had a long and happy life in store. Now, he committed more and more sinful acts, with the result that his sons died, he himself became sick and poor. Bewildered, he again asked the servant to look up his record. He learned from him that he had lost 20 percent of life and wealth because of intrigues which broke up families; another 20 percent for whoring and gambling, and still another 20 percent for slaughtering animals and other sins (2, 6a–b).

Mr. Chang saw in hell the calculation of Mr. Li's life. He had been destined to have a long life and sons in high positions. But as Mr. Li had been corrupt, he was re-destined to die early and his sons would have to pay a part of his sins because he had sinned too much (8, 22a–b).

Fate then is predestined but can be negatively or (in rare cases) positively changed by deeds during life. This theory restores the individual's responsibility and, in fact, pushes fate into the background as a decisive factor in life. Individual responsibility is stressed in still another connection:

Mr. Yao was a good but inactive official. During a flood in his district, only a part of the area suffered. Therefore, he was too lazy to request a tax reduction for his district and some people suffered much. He also had planned to build schools and orphanages, but did not do so because subaltern officials dissuaded him. His mother died and when she returned to life later, she told him that she had learned in hell that Yao would not have a son because he had not done what he had had the moral obligation to do (4, 16a–b).

[27] Karl Bünger, "The Punishment of Lunatics and Negligents according to Classical Chinese Law," *Monumenta Serica,* Vol. 9 (1950), pp. 1ff.

[28] Anthony Hulsewé, *Remnants of Han Law* (Leiden, 1955), p. 60. The *Yung-wan pi-chi* (chapter 3), a text from the late nineteenth century, discusses cases in which a man flirted with a girl or woman without raping her. The girl committed suicide. A law provided death penalty for this "crime." However, here the concept of "attenuating circumstances" has been introduced: if the man had flirted with her only by words or gestures, he will not be hanged. Full penalty has to be given when hands or feet had been used. A case discussed mentions a man who made an obscene gesture with his hand without touching the woman. He was hanged.

Conclusion

In many studies attempting to generalize, "Chinese society" has been seen as a unit. It is obvious that in studies of this type, the author based his conclusions on the writings of the Chinese upper class, especially on Confucianist texts. In contrast, many missionaries and observers who have lived in China but had no knowledge of Chinese literature and no access to upper-class life, have based their descriptions of "Chinese society" on their personal impressions, and therefore usually gave a picture of the lower-class society as it appeared to them in the light of their own standards and prejudices. Furthermore, a number of authors tried to fit together all the facts they knew and to construct a generalization which they wanted to compare with a generalized picture of Western society.

As Chinese traditional society was a hierarchically structured society built on a strong and conscious concept of class, anyone indulging in generalizations about China must take this fact into consideration. Traditional China was ruled by an educated elite, which believed that it had a right to rule because of its superior education and morality over the mass of ordinary people, stratified among themselves, who needed to be ruled. Practically all "respectable" literature and documents were written by the elite and for it, by upper-class authors for upper-class readers. This literature expressed the upper-class values, mainly Confucianism, and showed how individuals succeeded or failed to live up to these canons. While preserving its basic values intact over time, the Confucian value-system has, of course, changed in details during its more than two thousand years of existence.

According to Confucian standards of morality, the right to rule implies also the acceptance of certain obligations and duties, not only toward other members of the upper class, but also toward the population. One of these duties was to continue making attempts to raise the moral standards of the population by means of instruction. Not everybody could and should, according to traditional ideals, go to school and become a Confucianist; but certain "minimum requirements" should be fulfilled by everybody, even the humble, and we can observe that in the course of centuries the "minimum" was often raised, or at least attempts were made to raise the standards.

Seen from the viewpoint of the upper class, the medium of this instruction was religion, which, therefore, cannot quite be considered an "opiate for the people." While a truly educated Confucianist is basically an agnostic, he feels that the lower classes, who cannot reach the high Confucianist standards, need something easily understandable to act as an agent of moral control. Buddhist texts [1] are not normally written or translated by members of the upper class. Rather, they are written by foreigners and translated by marginal men: people with some education (i.e., Confucianist education), who had been unable or unwilling to fit into the Confucian system. These texts were read or memorized by the middle and lower classes and influenced their attitudes. Because of its precepts of morality, this literature was of value—seen from the viewpoint of the upper class. The common man was believed to be able to understand such books, which might influence him for the better. However, Confucianists fought against Buddhist values that were directly contrary to Confucianist social values, such as the Buddhist negation of reality, leading to depreciation of the family and of other social relations. From the eleventh or twelfth century on, such traits were no longer emphasized in the Buddhist mass religion, though they continued to exist. This happened at the same time when even Buddhist philosophy ceased to interest the elite, since Neo-Confucianism had begun to provide a sophisticated philosophy which was consistent with the contemporary needs of the upper class. Thus, from the twelfth century on, mass persecutions of Buddhists and severe attacks against its doctrine diminished: popular Buddhism had found its niche in the Confucian system as an institution of low-level moral education of the masses.

Similarly, the educated always scorned what I have called folk Taoism, and often fought and persecuted its adherents, believing that folk Taoism propagated among the masses values harmful to the Confucian system; yet they tolerated it with a sneer, also as a tool of moral mass education for those who had no better opportunity.

With the invention of printing, other mass literature, including novels, began to spread. At the same time, the urban middle classes developed a taste for drama and opera which, among the rural lower classes were

---

[1] Upper-class persons certainly read and appreciated the highly philosophical Buddhist treatises, but not for religious, only for philosophical, reasons. Taoist texts of high level are agnostic, too, and appeal, therefore, to Confucianists in certain moods.

imitated by shadow plays and marionette theater.[2] The upper class was against such light entertainment (although it was enjoyed by everyone in secret) and, unable to stop it, demanded that it at least serve educational purposes. Novels and plays should show in print or on the stage the rewards of moral behavior and the punishment of evil.

Thus, we find marginal members of the elite writing novels, plays, operas, or low-level religious-moralistic books, such as our *shan-shu*, for the reason that the masses presumably needed this kind of literature because they could not understand true literature. These authors were scholars who did not quite make it through the state examinations or who had bad luck in their career as officials, or scholars who were marginal psychologically although formally they were members of the system. Hoping that their writings would improve the moral attitudes of the masses, they defended their work as meritorious. We cannot analyze the minds of these writers; but it seems safe to assume that many of them were themselves not satisfied with Confucian morality and that they wrote plays and novels for their own satisfaction and pleasure, tacking on to their stories some trite moral only in order to be able to defend their compositions against the accusation of obscenity. But one can hardly prove that all of these popular writers had such feelings.

We have then, a "literature *for* the masses," not by the masses. There is, I think, no way to find out the true values of average people in traditional China. The common man could not or did not write. Foreigners who had contacts with ordinary people often could not understand them or misinterpreted their behavior. Besides, they had no true sample at their disposal. Often they may have described a correct picture—but there is no proof either for or against it.

It is mainly in the writings of foreigners that we find the stress upon shame in Chinese society; it is they who stated that the Chinese were typically afraid of "losing their face." It is they who reported many cases of suicide because of loss of face, or of samsonitic suicide, suicide in

---

[2] There are two types of puppet show. The *pu-tai-hsi* (bag play), with puppets which are operated from below with the hand, is supposedly not more than 300 years old and originated in Ch'üan-chou, Fukien (*T'ai-wan feng-wu*, 10 [1960] No. 5, p. 6; and *T'ai-wan feng t'u*, No. 153 [1952]), and the plays are derived from ordinary plays. The *k'ui-lei-hsi* had always a religious character and was played during religious meetings (well described in the Ming drama *Lan Ts'ai-ho*). The character of the plays is not known; to my knowledge no text has yet been published. As the word *k'ui-lei* seems to be non-Chinese, the relation between *k'ui-lei* and Turkish *kukla* and the supposedly Greek root from which *kukla* is derived, has aroused much interest. Already Plato mentions marionettes. A. Bombaci, "On Ancient Turkish Dramatic Performances" (in D. Sinor, *Aspects of Altaic Civilization* [Bloomington, 1963], pp. 87–117), raised the question that gypsies might have brought *k'ui-lei* plays to Central Asia, a theory which has also been mentioned in relation to Korea, where similar plays occur.

order to punish another person after one's death as a ghost, or to cause through suicide endless difficulties or even punishment [3] to the other person. But in the Chinese literature used here, including also the short stories, I did not once find the phrase "losing face"; and there was no clear case of suicide because of shame alone. As far as shame was involved in the suicide cases, it came as a secondary element, added to the element of sin. There was also no clear case of samsonitic suicide in more than a hundred reports of suicide, even though the books on sin indicate its existence and condemn it.

The reason for this contrast may be that, in this study, we have relied upon upper-class literature *for* the masses, not on statements *by* the masses. I did not study what the common man thought about shame versus guilt and how he behaved in relevant situations in traditional China, because there are no reliable literary data for such an investigation. Educated authors have sometimes written about the masses, but usually only to criticize immoral or outrageous acts which may not be at all typical or widespread. Besides, these reports are *about* common people and still not *by* them.

This study, then, is a study of moral values which the upper class thought the lower classes should have or which the leaders hoped the masses would internalize. It is conceivable that the common people in traditional China indeed had more or less internalized these values, although it remains to be proved.

Average traditional Chinese who cannot be called Confucianist were educated then toward an internalization of guilt, mainly by popularized Buddhism and folk Taoism. Shame can be regarded as an amoral principle: everything is all right, as long as an action running counter to the rules of "correct" behavior remains secret. Public exposure and the fear of it are the means of social control; internalization of moral values is not necessary. In our religious texts the stress is on internalization of guilt: moral values and behavioral rules exist, and any violation, whether known or secret, whether done on purpose or unwillingly, is sin. The deities are aware of every violation and punish it. If shame is involved, it may be compared to the shame felt by a criminal whose crime was

[3] Hu Hsien-chin, "The Chinese Concepts of Face," *American Anthropologist,* Vol. 46 (1944), pp. 46–47, discusses a case of a suicide of a girl who had been jilted by her lover, a college student. The student was severely punished for his irresponsibility, to promise marriage and not to keep the promise. According to her analysis, the student's behavior caused many discussions and made him lose face completely. According to the *shan-shu* the girl has committed a sin; but so did the boy.

discovered; what is decisive is the crime; the shame, not anticipated and not felt until later, is only an additional element.

A shame society, by definition, is based upon a system of exclusively social values; there is neither sin nor guilt. There may be punishment, but the socializing factor is shame. In contrast, the concepts of sin and guilt are transcendental and social concepts; guilt and punishment are the socializing factors. While a value-system based only upon social values tends to be relativistic and open to change, a value-system built upon transcendental values tends to be monolithic, absolutistic, and opposed to change. Both shame and guilt occur in stratified societies, but guilt does not fit too well with certain forms of egalitarian societies. For example, in egalitarian societies of the West, which tend to be multiple societies, different sectors of the society may have different value-systems. A multiple society with different value-systems, and with, therefore, a relativistic attitude toward good and bad, may develop anomic behavior, but a stratified society with one guilt-based value-system cannot even conceive the possibility of anomie. In theory an individual in such a society can never be in doubt as to the right way to act, since there exists only one code of behavior. Chinese thought has softened the rigor of this doctrine by admitting that not everybody can be expected to fully live up to the highest standards. Incidentally, Christianity has taken the same attitude in practice. It is for this reason of the absoluteness of the moral code that the Chinese literature contains no cases of anomic suicide. But we found cases of suicide which are tragic, for a Chinese as well as for us. A tragic situation may arise from a conflict between different *value-systems,* as for instance in modern Japan where the youth begins to adhere to the Western form of love, marriage, and premarital relations, while the parent generation still largely adheres to the Chinese form of arranged marriage, that is, where marriage was a tie between two families, not between two individuals. Therefore, in Japan, we find tragic suicides of young couples who find themselves caught between the two moral systems. But in traditional China, tragic situations arose from conflicts within *one* value-system, as they did in Greece and everywhere else. For example, a person had either unknowingly or even against his will violated a norm and was punished for this; or a person was caught in a situation in which he could live up to the requirements of a high norm only by violating another high norm. There were also simpler dilemma situations in which any step led necessarily to a violation of norms, with no way out. A conflict between two norms was usually not insoluble, because norms had been arranged hierarchically, at least in post-Sung time, and everyone in the situation would have known what to do.

Before this time, however, there were still two great insoluble conflicts, because the values involved had not yet been assigned differential places in the hierarchy of norms. The first of these conflicts was between piety (in our case: to remain alive in order to be able to take care of the parents) and loyalty (to fight until death for the ruler); it was eventually solved by the decision that loyalty to the ruler ranks first because it is he who makes social life possible. The second conflict was between the duty to revenge the murder of a parent and the law of the state prohibiting murder; it was solved by the decision that the state would undertake the revenge.

Seen from the outside, Chinese society was, of course, not a unified, but always a multiple society, besides being stratified. We know, for instance, that the aborigines who once inhabited most of Central and South China had their own value-systems and that great conflicts arose when the Chinese imposed their norms upon them. For example, just as in modern Japan, the imposition of a new—the Chinese—marriage system, which replaced the free marriage system of the aborigines, caused a series of tragic love suicides.

It may be rare that shame is an instrument of socialization in any lower class, although it seems neither impossible nor improbable. But it could very well be that the upper class of a society typically attempts or propagates socialization of the masses by a system based upon guilt, while relying upon shame as the socializing factor for themselves. In other words, perhaps Confucianism, as the ideology of China's elite of the traditional period, was built upon the principle of shame. Do Confucianists, then, in fact bring up their children by using shame as the main socializing factor? We do not have field research upon which we could rely. Without doubt Confucian texts often use the concept of shame. Our collection of short stories contained a number of examples of shame, and many, though not all, of these stories were written by upper-class authors for upper-class readers.

However, the main category of stories involving shame dealt primarily with sins. The element of shame came in only when the sinful act became public knowledge. Only the last category of cases had nothing to do with sin and dealt with shame alone. The persons involved, almost always men and members of the upper class, indeed "lost face" because they had indulged in behavior which was contrary to the behavior expected of a person high in social status and rank. This seems, indeed, to be the main function of shame in Chinese traditional society. Shame involves loss of social status. Shameful actions are those which are inconsistent with the status of the actor; they are not necessarily sinful, but they may even be sinful in addition. Here, we must truly go back directly to Confucius. One of the main points of his system was indeed that in his opinion the old aristocrats, the "knights" of old China, had lost their right to be rulers and leaders, because their actions were inconsistent with the duties involved in their status. Confucius set forth the ideal of the new elite: not persons born into the upper class should be rulers, but persons entering a new upper class because of superior moral behavior. Consequently, he reworded (according to an old and good tradition) the annals of his home country, Lu, by evaluating every action of a member of the upper class and by dealing out "praise and blame" (*pao-pien*). Thus, a war could be called "King X punished Country Y" or "castigated" or "pacified" or "attacked" or "assailed," according to whether the war of aggression was, in Confucius's evaluation, a moral one or not. Here is an example of extremely shameful behavior: to serve more than one ruler, as did Feng Tao in the tenth century,[4] was not a sin in the religious sense, it was not even a crime in the legal sense; but, as a trusted minister, a member of the elite, he was expected to remain loyal, since loyalty has been one of the cardinal Confucian virtues. Yet he was selfish enough to serve the next ruler, whoever he turned out to be. Feng Tao was, for the eleventh century Confucianist at least, the man without honor, the symbol of a man without shame.

Shame is felt when social obligations or rules, even simple formal rules of manners, are violated. Any such violation inevitably involves also the family of the violator. Books on the education of upper-class women, written by women, speak much about shame, because any mistake in daily manners by a wife allows conclusions upon her upbringing and shames her family. The family should have taught the girl the manners consistent with her future status, and the family is blamed if the girl did not learn proper behavior. Her mistakes also shame her husband's family because, even if she had been insufficiently educated, the husband's family should have seen to it that her manners improved.

In all these cases, shame is the reverse of honor. The loss of honor, that is, the loss of gentleman status, was as important in Confucian thought and practice as in the aristocratic societies of the Near East, Central Asia, and old Europe. Confucianism, then, was based on the same maxim as was the old European society: "noblesse oblige"; in fact,

---

[4] Lived 882–954; he served twelve emperors belonging to several different dynasties. Wang Gung-wu, "Feng Tao: An Essay on Confucian Loyalty" (in Arthur Wright, *Confucianism and Chinese Civilization* [New York, 1964], pp. 188–210), has shown that his contemporaries had a high opinion of Feng Tao and that, judging from the conditions of his time, his behavior was hardly reprehensible.

only with this maxim can an upper class continue to claim its right and feel justified to rule.

The predominance of the concept of shame and the absence of sin in Confucianism do not allow the conclusion that Confucianists had no feelings about immorality. They did, but in the Confucian system immoral acts were conceived as "crimes," to be punished. However, Confucianists always maintained that laws are essentially for the lower classes and should not be necessary for the gentleman. He should be motivated and guided by his concepts of honor and propriety, which are rooted in his concepts of class and class obligations. Crimes were considered violations of the cosmic order. The social order is simultaneously a part of, and parallel to, the cosmic order, logically consistent with it and not based upon the whims of a deity or a pantheon. A true Confucianist is not afraid of deities, ghosts, or spirits, but he is afraid of upsetting the cosmic or social order. Like the religious person, he has his code in his heart, he has internalized his social code. He feels ashamed not only in the case of exposure, but even if no one knows of his bad actions—or at least he is expected to feel this way.

The definition of shame as the reverse side of honor is consistent with a hierarchically structured class society. The code of honor of the elite is one of the ways by which social change is inhibited, particularly the degeneration of the upper class, which by necessity would lead to the assumption of power by another class. Therefore, no member of the upper class should bring himself into a shameful situation, because this would mean loss of status for himself and possibly for his entire class.

We can say, then, that the traditional elite of China had an ideology in which shame played an important role, but not in the conventional sense of amoral shame. On the contrary, shame in Confucianism was a moral concept and was internalized, together with the precepts of the code of social behavior. In essence, then, shame and guilt operate in the same way.

Does such an analysis allow any conclusions about social change in China? On the one side, we have seen that originally foreign Buddhist concepts of sin were adapted in China, until the resulting folk religion finally included many elements of Confucian thought, so that it became, so to speak, a "Confucianism for the middle and lower classes," recognized as a means of moral uplift of the lower classes.

On the other side, one gets the impression from the Chinese literature of the nineteenth century that the elite lost its sense of shame, that "gentlemen" indulged freely in all kinds of behavior that was shameful as well as sinful. One has the feeling that the upper class also lost its sense of mission, duty, and responsibility. This occurred at the same time that the *shan-shu* spread widely and became more and more violent in their descriptions of sins and punishments, assailing especially the elite for disbelief and misbehavior. At the same time, this was the period when Christianity gained strength in China and underlined in its own way the concept of guilt while dismissing the concept of shame. Did the elite begin to feel estranged from its shame-oriented code of behavior and to take over the more democratic or, perhaps better, egalitarian concept of guilt? In any event, it is curious to see that Communist China seems to come back to the old dual system: guilt is stressed for the masses and in general—where guilt is defined as a violation of the quasi-religious Marxist doctrine; and the new ruling class, the party members, are under special higher obligations, which are derived from their high rank and social status above the masses.

Glossary of Chinese Terms

Ch'eng-huang 城隍
chia-tse 甲子
ch'ih 恥
Ching-kung temple 景公寺
ching-t'u 淨土
Ch'ing-t'u 清土
Chiu-hua 九華山

Ho-ta 合大
hsiao 孝
hsiu 羞
hua 化

ju 辱

keng-shen 庚申
kuo 過
Kuan-ti 關帝
Kuan 觀
Kuan-yin 觀音
Kuang-han-tien 廣寒殿

li 禮
lien-hsin 廉心

miao 廟
ming 命
Mu-lien 木蓮（目蓮）

nai-ho 奈何
Niu-t'ou 牛頭

P'an-lung mountain 蟠龍山
pao-pien 褒貶
Pei-chi ti-yü 北极
pi-chi 筆紀
ping 丙

san-yüan 三元
sen-lo 森羅
shan-shu 善書
sheng-yü 聖諭
shih-lien 失臉
sih 寺

Ta-ti 大帝
T'ai-shan 泰山
tao 道
ti-yü 地獄
Ti-tsang 地藏
Ti-tsang-en 地藏菴
ting 丁
ts'an-k'ui 慙愧
tsui 罪
Tung-yüeh hsing-kung
東嶽行宮

127

Tung-yüeh miao 東嶽廟

Wang-hsiang-t'ai 望鄉台

Wang szu ch'eng 枉死城

wei 穢

wu-la 五臘

yang 陽

Yen-lo wang 閻羅王

yin 陰

yü 獄

Yü Huang-ti 玉皇帝

yüan 院

Bibliography

Arranged alphabetically according to authors for modern and Western works; according to titles for Chinese texts.

Barnouw, Victor. *Culture and Personality* (Homewood, 1963).

Beal, Samuel. *A Catena of Buddhist Scriptures from the Chinese* (London, 1871).

Beauclair, Inez de. "A Miao Tribe of Southern Kweichow and its Cultural Configuration," *Bulletin of the Institute of Ethnology,* No. 10 (Taipei, 1960), pp. 127–205.

Benedict, Ruth. *The Chrysanthemum and the Sword* (London, 1947).

Bijutsu Kenkyu 美術研究 (Tokyo, periodical).

Bombaci, A. "On Ancient Turkish Dramatic Performances," in D. Sinor, *Aspects of Altaic Civilization* (Bloomington, 1963), pp. 87–117.

Cavan, Ruth. *Suicide* (Chicago, 1928).

Chavannes, Edouard. *Le T'ai chan* (Paris, 1910).

Cheng-fa nien-ch'u ching (*Vajraśekhara yiga*) 正法念處經 . Reprinted in *Taishô Tripitaka,* Vol. 17, pp. 27ff; another text in Vol. 17, pp. 92ff.

Chi-szu chen pao 己巳真宝 . Reprinted in *Shê-sheng tsung-yao.*

Chia-i sheng-yen 甲乙剩言 . Author Hu Ying 胡應 . Ming time. Selection in *Li-tai hsiao-shuo pi-chi hsüan,* Vol. 1.

Chien-teng hsien-hua 剪燈新話 . Author Ch'ü Yo 瞿佑 (1341–1427).

Ch'ih p'o-tse chuan 癡婆子傳 . Author unknown (Library of Institute of Sex Research).

Chin-ku ch'i-kuan 今古奇觀 . Author unknown. Ming time.

Ch'iu-yü-wan sui-pi 秋雨盦隨筆 . Author Liang Shao-jen 梁紹壬 . Early nineteenth century. Edition: *Pi-chi hsiao-shuo ta-kuan* (Shanghai).

Chou-kung chieh-meng 周公解夢 . Author unknown. Edition Chulin Press (Hsin-chu, Taiwan, 1960).

Ch'ü-hai tsung-mu t'i-yao 曲海總目提要 . Early eighteenth century. Edition Peking, Jen-min wen-hsüeh, 1959.

Chung-tse pi-p'ou 種子秘剖 . Author unknown. Reprinted in *Shê-sheng tsung-yao.*

Clarke, G. W., "The Yü-li, or Precious Records," *Journal of the Royal Asiatic Society, China Branch,* Vol. 28, No. 2 (1893), pp. 233–400.

Cormack, Margaret L. *She Who Rides a Peacock* (New York, 1961).

Doré, Henry. *Recherches sur les Superstitions en Chine.* 18 vols. (Shanghai, 1911–1938).

Durkheim, Emile. *Suicide* (Glencoe, 1951).

Eberhard, Wolfram. "Chinese Regional Stereotypes," *Asian Survey,* 5 (1965), No. 12, pp. 596–608.

——. *Die chinesische Novelle* (*Artibus Asiae,* Supplement No. 9. Ascona, 1948).

——. *Die Lokalkulturen im alten China.* 2 vols. (Leiden and Peking, 1943).

——. "Religious Activities and Religious Books in Modern China," *Zeitschrift für Missionswissenschaft,* No. 4 (1965), pp. 260–269.

——. *Typen chinesischer Volksmärchen* (*Folklore Fellows Communications,* No. 120. Helsinki, 1937).

——. *Volksmärchen aus Südost-China* (*Folklore Fellows Communications,* No. 127. Helsinki, 1941).

Eichhorn, Werner. "Einige Bemerkungen zum Aufstand des Chang Chio und zum Staate des Chang Lu," *Deutsche Akademie d.Wiss., Berlin, Inst.für Orientforschung,* 3 (1955), pp. 291–327.

Elliott, Alan J. *Chinese Spirit-Medium Cults in Singapore* (London, 1955).

Edwards, Evangeline D. *Chinese Prose Literature of the T'ang Period.* 2 vols. (London, 1937).

Elwin, Verrier. *Myths of Middle India* (Oxford, 1949).

Erh-ju 耳郵 . Author "Yang-shu-weng" 羊朱翁 . Manchu period. Edition: *Pi-chi hsiao-shuo ta-kuan.*

Erh-shih lu 耳食錄 . Author Lo Chün 樂鈞 . Nineteenth century. Edition: *Pi-chi hsiao-shuo ta-kuan.*

Fo-shuo shih-pa ni-li ching 佛説十八泥犁經. Reprinted in *Taishô Tripitaka.*

Fo-shuo tsui-yeh ying-pao (chiao-hua ti-yü) ching 佛説罪業應報. Reprinted in *Taishô Tripitaka.*

Folklore Studies (Peking, periodical).

Franke, Herbert. "Eine Novellensammlung der frühen Ming-Zeit: Das Chien-teng hsien-hua des Ch'ü Yu," *Zeitschr.d. Deutschen Morgenländischen Gesellschaft,* Vol. 108, No. 2 (1958), pp. 338–382.

Freud, Sigmund. *Civilization and its Discontents* (New York, 1930).

Grube, Wilhelm. *Pekinger Volkskunde. (Veröffentl. d. kgl. Museums f. Vökerkunde Berlin.* Vol. 7, Nos. 1–4).

van Gulik, Robert H. *Sexual Life in Ancient China* (Leiden, 1961).

Heissig, Walther. *Helden-, Höllenfahrts- und Schelmengeschichten der Mongolen* (Berlin, 1962).

Hitson (Weidman), Hazel. "Family Patterns and Paranoidal Personality Structure in Boston and Burma." Unpublished Ph.D. dissertation, Radcliffe College, 1959.

Ho-sha chi 合紗記. Drama by Shih P'an 史磐. Ming time (cf. *Ch'ü-hai*).

Ho Ting-jui. "East Asian Themes in Folktales of the Formosan Aborigines," *Asian Folklore Studies,* 23 (1964), No. 2.

Ho-tung chi 河東記. Author Liu K'ai 柳開. Tenth century. Quoted in *T'P'KCh.*

Honigman, John J. *Understanding Culture* (New York, 1963).

Hsiang mei sih 香梅寺. Drama. See W. Grube, *Volkskunde,* p. 79.

Hsiang-yin-lou pin-t'an 香飲樓賓談. Author Lu Ch'ang-ch'un 陸長春. Manchu period. Edition: *Pi-chi hsiao-shuo ta-kuan.*

Hsing-hsin-li hsüeh. See P'an Kuang-tan.

Hsing-shan fu-pao p'ien 行善福報篇. Author unknown. Printed around 1875.

Hsiao-ching 孝經. Author unknown. Pre-Christian period.

Hsiao-tse chuan 孝子傳. Author Hsü Kuang 徐廣. Fourth century. Quoted in *T'P'KCh* and *T'P'YL.*

Hsieh-to 諧鐸 . Author Shen Ch'i-feng 沈起鳳 . Manchu period. Edition: *Pi-chi hsiao-shuo ta-kuan.*

Hsiu-wen chi 修文記 . Drama by T'u Lung 屠隆 . Ming time (cf. *Ch'ü-hai*).

Hsu, Francis L. K., *Clan, Caste, and Club* (New York, 1963).

—— ed. *Psychological Anthropology* (Homewood, 1961).

——. "Some Aspects of Personality of Chinese as Revealed by the Rorschach Test," *Journal of Projective Techniques,* 13 (1949), No. 3, pp. 285–301.

——. *Under the Ancestors Shadows* (New York, 1948).

Hsü Po-wu-chih 續博物志. Author Li Shih 李石 . Tenth century.

Hsü Tse-pu-yü 續子不語 . Author Yüan Mei 袁枚 . Eighteenth century.

Hu Hsien-chin. "The Chinese Concept of Face," *American Anthropologist,* 46 (1944), pp. 45–66.

Hua-yo shan 滑油山 . Drama. Author unknown.

Hulsewé, Anthony. *Remnants of Han Law* (Leiden, 1955).

I-chien-chih 夷堅志 . Author Hung Mai 洪邁 . Sung period. Edition: *Pi-chi hsiao-shuo ta-kuan.*

I-wen tsung-lu 異聞總錄. Author unknown. Sung period. Edition: *Pi-chi hsiao-shuo ta-kuan.*

Jacobs, Melville. *The Content and Style of an Oral Literature* (New York, 1959).

Julien, Stanislas. *Livre des récompenses et des peines* (Paris, 1835).

Kaplan, Bert, ed. *Studying Personality Cross-culturally* (Evanston, 1961).

Kölner Zeitschrift f. Soziologie und Sozial-Psychologie (periodical).

Körner, Brunhild. *Die religiöse Welt der Bäuerin in Nord-China* (Stockholm, 1959).

Kraeling, Carl H., and R. M. Adams. *City Invincible* (Chicago, 1960).

Kuang-i-chi 廣異記 . Author Tai Chün-fou 戴君孚 . Quoted in *T'P'KCh.*

Kuang-yang tsa-chi 廣陽雜記. Author Liu Chi-chuang 劉繼莊 . Manchu period. Edition: *Pi-chi hsiao-shuo ta-kuan.*

Kui-tung 鬼董 . Author: Mr. Shen 沈氏 Sung period.

Lan Ts'ai-ho 藍采和 . Drama by Lai Chi-chih 來集之 . Seventeenth century (cf. *Ch'ü-hai*).

Leach, Edmund R. *Political Systems of Highland Burma* (Cambridge, England, 1954).

Leng-lu tsa-chih 冷廬雜識 . Author Lu Ching-an 陸敬安 . Manchu period. Edition: *Pi-chi hsiao-shuo ta-kuan*.

Li-chi 禮紀 . Author unknown.

Li-tai hsiao-shuo pi-chi hsüan: Ming 歷代筆紀小說選：明 . 2 vols. Commercial Press (Hong Kong, n.d.).

Liao-chai chih-i 聊齋志異 . Author P'u Sung-ling 蒲松齡 . Early eighteenth century.

Lo-Pu miao-jung 羅卜描容 . Folk drama, published in *Chung-kuo ti-fang hsi-ch'ü*, Anhui 中國地方戲曲,安徽省 , No. 43, pp. 967f.

Lo Yin hsiang-pao hsin-ko 落陰相褒新歌 . Folk booklet, no author, in Fukien dialect. Published in Taichung (Taiwan), Showa eighth year. Jui-ch'eng Press.

Long, Howard R. *The People of Mushan* (Columbia, Miss., 1960).

Lowe, Carrington M. "The Study of the Nature of Guilt in Psychopathology," *Dissertation Abstracts,* 22 (1961), pp. 909–910.

Lu Lou-sha. *Hsing-yü t'ao-lun ta-kuan* 性欲討論大觀 (Shanghai, 1926). (Library of the Institute of Sex Research).

Lung-hua hui 龍華會 . Drama by Wang Hsiang-ch'ien 王翔千 Early Manchu period (cf. *Ch'ü-hai*).

Lynd, Helen M. *On Shame and the Search for Identity* (New York, 1961), paperback edition.

Mai-yü chi 埋憂集 . Author Chu Mei-shu 朱梅叔 . Nineteenth century. Edition: *Pi-chi hsiao-shuo ta-kuan*.

Mead, Margaret, and R. Métraux. *Study of Culture at a Distance* (New York, 1953).

Meng-liang lu 夢梁錄 . Author Wu Tse-mu 吳自牧 . Sung period. Edition: *Pi-chi hsiao-shuo ta-kuan*.

Min-pao-chi 冥報記 . Author T'ang Lin 唐臨 . T'ang period. Edition: *Taishô Tripitaka*.

Mo-yü-lu 墨餘錄 . Author Mao Hsiang-lin 毛祥麟 . Nineteenth century. Edition: *Pi-chi hsiao-shuo ta-kuan*.

Monumenta Serica (Peking, periodical).

Mu-lien chiu-mu 目蓮救母. Drama. Author unknown. (Parts are mentioned in G. Jacob, *Das chinesische Schattentheater,* p. 20).

Neng-kai-chai man-lu 能改齋漫錄. Author Wu Tseng 吳曾 . Sung period. Edition: *Pi-chi hsiao-chuo ta-kuan.*

Niida Noboru 仁井田陞. *T'ang Law (Tôryô Shûi)* 唐令拾遺 . (Tokyo, 1933).

Nü-hung sha 女紅紗. Drama by Lai Chi-chih 來集之. Seventeenth century (cf. *Ch'ü-hai*).

P'an Kuang-tan (Quentin Pan) 潘光旦 , transl. *Hsing-hsin-li hsüeh* 性心理學 . (Annotated transl. of Havelock Ellis, *Psychology of Sex*), Commercial Press (Shanghai, 1948).

Pei-p'ing huai-ku 北平懷古. In Ch'i Ju-shan 齊如山 , *Ch'i Ju-shan ch'üan chi* 齊如山全集 , Vol. 7 (Taipei, 1964).

Penzer, Norman M. *Poison-damsels and other Essays* (London, 1952).

Sakai, T. *Studies of Chinese shan-shu, Popular Books on Morality* (Tokyo, 1960).

Shan-chü hsin-hua 山居新話 . Author Yang Yü 楊瑀. Fourteenth century.

Shê-sheng tsung-yao 攝生總要 . Edition of 1638 by Hung Chu-yo. (Inst. of Sex Research, Bloomington).

Shyrok, John K. *The Temples of Anking* (Paris, 1931).

Shu-ching 書經 . Author unknown.

Shu-i-chi 述異記 . Author perhaps Jen Fang 任昉. Fourth century or later.

Sou-shen-chi 搜神記 . Author Kan Pao 干宝 . Fourth century? Quoted in *T'P'YL* and *T'P'KCh.*

Sou-shen hou-chi 搜神後記 . Author supposedly T'ao Ch'ien 陶潛. Fourth century? Quoted in *T'P'YL* and *T'P'KCh.*

Stephens, William N. *The Oedipus Complex: Cross-cultural Evidence* (Glencoe, 1962).

Su-nü-ching 素女經 . Author unknown. Reprinted in *Shuang-mei ching en ts'ung-shu* 雙梅景闇叢書 . Here used reprint in *Yü-fang pi-chüeh,* undated Taiwan print by the Wu-ching-t'ang Press.

Su-t'an 蘇談 . Author Yang Hsün-chi 楊循吉 . Ming period. (Excerpts in *Li-tai hsiao-shuo pi-chi hsüan,* Ming.)

T'ai-shang kan-ying p'ien 太上感應篇 . (Quoted in next text.)

T'ai-shang pao-fa t'u-shuo 太上宝法圖説 . Edited by Huang Cheng-yüan 黃正元 . 1903 edition.

Taishô Tripitaka 大正三藏經 . Tokyo.

T'ai-wan feng-t'u 台灣風土 . Folkloristic supplement to the paper *Kung-lun pao* 公論報 , Nos. 1–195 (1948–1954).

T'ai-wan feng-wu 台灣風物 (periodical).

T'ang hua-tuan 唐畫斷 . Author Chu Ching-hsüan 朱景玄 . Quoted in *T'P'KCh.*

Tomita, Kojiro. *Portfolio of Chinese Paintings* (Boston, 1933).

T'P'KCh: T'ai-p'ing kuang-chi 太平廣記 . Author Li Fang 李昉 . Tenth century. Edition: *Pi-chi hsiao-shuo ta-kuan.*

T'P'YL: T'ai-p'ing yü-lan 太平御覽 . Author Li Fang 李昉 . Tenth century. Edition: *Sih-pu ts'ung-k'an,* Commercial Press (Shanghai).

Ti-kung-an 狄公案 . Author unknown. Eighteenth century. See R. H. van Gulik, *Dee Goong An* (Tokyo, 1949).

Ts'an t'ung ch'i 參同契 . Supposed author Wei Po-yang 魏伯陽 . Second century.

Tseng Erh-niang shao hao-hsiang ko 曾二娘燒好香歌 Popular ballad, no author. Printed in Chia-i hsien, Taiwan, Showa 9. Fukien dialect.

Tso-chuan 左傳 . Compiler supposedly Tso-ch'iu Ming 左丘明 .

Tun-huang pien-wen chi 焞煌變文集 . Compilers Wang Chung-min and others 王重民 . Peking, Jen-min wen-hsüeh, 1957. 2 vols.

T'un-k'u lan-yen 遯窟讕言 . Author Wang T'ao 王韜 . Late nineteenth century. Edition: Ta-ta Press, Shanghai.

Tung-hsüan-tse 洞玄子 . Author unknown. Perhaps seventh century. Edition: *Yü-fang pi-chüeh* (see above under *Su-nü-ching*).

Tung-ming pao-chi 洞冥宝記 . Author unknown. Undated edition in 2 vols. Printed in Taipei, no printing press mentioned.

Turrettini, François. *Le livre des récompenses et des peines* (Génève, 1889).

Wan-li yeh-huo pien 萬曆野獲編 . Author Shen Te-fu 沈德符 . Sixteenth century. Edition: Chung-hua Press (Shanghai, 1959).

Wan shih tsu 萬事足 . Drama by Feng Meng-lung 馮夢龍 Ming period (cf. *Ch'ü-hai*).

Wang Sung-hsing. "Fairy Tales of the Vataan Ami," *Bulletin of the Institute of Ethnology,* No. 14 (1962), pp. 95–127.

Wang Ts'ui-ch'iao chuan 王翠翹傳

Welch, Holmes. *Taoism: The Parting of the Way* (Boston, 1966), paperback edition.

Woo Chan Cheng. *Érotologie de la Chine* (Paris, 1963).

Wright, Arthur. *Confucianism and Chinese Civilization* (New York, 1964).

Wu Hsi-chung. "A Comparative Study of the Problem of Suicide," *Shêhui tao-chih* 社會導指 Vol. 1, No. 2 (Taipei, 1964), pp. 21–28.

Wu-lin chiu-shih 武林舊事 . Author Chou Mi 周密 . Sung period. Edition: *Pi-chi hsiao-shuo ta-kuan.*

Yang-chou hua-fang lu 楊州畫舫錄 . Author Li Tou 李斗 . Eighteenth century. Chung-hua Press (Peking, 1960).

Yeh-k'o ts'ung-shu 野客叢書 . Author Wang Mou 王懋 . Sung period. Edition: *Pi-chi hsiao-shuo ta-kuan.*

Yeh-t'an sui-lu 夜談 . Author unknown. Nineteenth century. Edition: *Pi-chi hsiao-shuo ta-kuan.*

Yo-ming-lu 幽明錄 . Author Liu I-ch'ing 劉義慶 . Quoted in *T'P'KCh.*

Yü-fang pi-chüeh 玉房秘決 . Author unknown. Inside title: *Shuang-mei-ching en ts'ung-shu.* Taipei print, no year, Wu-ching t'ang Press.

Yüeh-wei ts'ao-t'ang pi-chi 閱微草堂筆記 . Author Chi Yün . Early nineteenth century. Edition: Ta-ta Press (Shanghai, 1934).

Yü-li (chih) pao ch'ao 玉曆(至)宝鈔. Author unknown. Various editions. Used (a) Shanghai, I-hua t'ang Press, approx. 1923; (b) Taichung, Jui-ch'eng Press, 1963; (c) Taipei print, 1954, no press mentioned.

Yung-hsien-chai pi-chi 庸閒齋筆記 . Author Ch'en Ch'i-yüan 陳其元. Manchu period. Edition: *Pi-chi hsiao-shuo ta-kuan.*

Yung-wan pi-chi 庸盦筆記 . Author Hsüeh Fu-ch'eng 薛福成 . Nineteenth century. Edition: *Pi-chi hsiao-shuo ta-kuan* (Shanghai)

Index

GUILT AND SIN
IN TRADITIONAL CHINA

By Wolfram Eberhard

Well known for his earlier studies in sociology, sinology and folklore, Mr. Eberhard here draws on his knowledge of all three fields, marshalling fresh data and insights with characteristic orginality.

Some social-psychologists distinguish between human societies that employ concepts of guilt to cope with non-conformist or deviant behavior and other societies that employ concepts of shame for this purpose. In this sense, China has usually been regarded as a "shame society." However, Mr. Eberhard finds that, although shame appears to have played an appreciable role in the socialization of children in traditional China and may retain its importance to the present day, its significance has apparently differed from one social class to another.

Mr. Eberhard examines several types of Chinese literature (including notably the *shan-shu*) that have been popular for at least 1,500 years, and draws on them to show how concepts of sin and retribution have changed during this time. He also analyzes a representative collection of short stories, spanning some 800 years, in order to determine how the moral values held by their educated authors differed from those of the more popular writers. His findings along the way not only offer new insights into the value system that was inculcated among the lower classes in traditional China but also suggest implications regarding values characteristic of contemporary China.

Mr. Eberhard is Professor of Sociology at the University of California, Berkeley, and is the author of many books, including *Social Mobility in Traditional China, Folktales of China,* and *Settlement and Social Change in Asia.*